Starting Simple

Starting Simple

Conversations about the Way We Live

Bob Sitze

THE
ALBAN
INSTITUTE

Herndon, Virginia
www.alban.org

The Alban Institute
2121 Cooperative Way, Suite 100
Herndon, VA 20171

Cover design by Spark Design, LLC.

Library of Congress Cataloging-in-Publication Data

Sitze, Bob.
  Starting simple : conversations about the way we live / Bob Sitze.
     p. cm.
  ISBN-13: 978-1-56699-354-8
  1. Simplicity—Religious aspects—Christianity. I. Title.
  BV4647.S48S58 2007
  241'.4—dc22
                                    2007035682

   11   10   09   08   07   VG   1   2   3   4   5

*To Ed and Vera Sitze, whose storied simple living
still shapes my entire world.*

Contents

~~

Preface

As Western civilization turns the world into a fast-moving trash truck, the body of literature about simple living grows quickly. I have noticed at least two varieties of writing about simplicity. The first kind presents earnest propositions about simplicity itself. What simple living consists of, why we should value it, what will happen if people don't start living this way. "Think your way into acting" is the operating principle.

Another genre of writing collects helpful hints, categorized listings of specific actions people might take to change their lifestyle. Some of the hints are handy, others hard, but all of them are helpful starters. "Act your way into thinking" is the guiding methodology for this kind of resource.

What some folks—myself included—are trying to find is still another way to move simple living into the mainstream of thought and behavior in congregations. We are trying to invent resources that help God's people leapfrog over some of the roadblocks and pitfalls that keep them from living simply. (An example of one of our questions: What actually animates minds and bodies?)

Many members of your congregation yearn for simpler lives. They see themselves as just a little strange, moving against the mainstream of American consumerism, odd ducks in a world of too much, too fast, too many. My hope is that by reading this book you will strengthen your resolve to work alongside them in untying the Gordian knot of civilization: how to live joyfully and justly without destroying ourselves and the planet.

As of this writing, more than 6.5 million Web entries include some combination of the words simple living. *More than 13 million entries include "get rich" in their wording.*

You can use this book to help the people of your congregation:

- Learn what the Scriptures have to say about living a godly life in these times.
- Find ways to repent about the ways in which their schedules are spinning out of control, their bank accounts leaking, their stuff rotting, their relationships thinning.
- Gather courage to change the ways they think and live.
- Speak and listen to the struggles of others with honesty and respect.

This is a practical book, approachable and respectful of your leadership. Each chapter includes "asides"—notes at the top of the page that are filled with thoughtful quotes, short stories, and activities. You will probably want to scribble in the margins, reread some sections, stuff clippings into the book, pray about what the readings evoke in your spirit.

To make best use of this book, think about who pays attention to you and to whom you pay attention. That might be the start of some first-ever, straightforward exchanges about questions like these:

- How long can things keep going on this way without collapsing?
- Why are people living so fast, collecting so much stuff, working so hard?
- What else could I be doing with my life?

*Don't worry about tomorrow. It will take care of itself. You have
enough to worry about today.*
—Matthew 6:34

- Where is all this leading?
- What *would* Jesus do in this situation?

Use this book to spark conversations, invite sharing, make decisions, ask for forgiveness, witness at work, or encourage others who are ready to change. In your congregation, this may be a good guide for small group discussions, family negotiations, or formal programming.

Enjoy what you read here; enjoy even more putting these ideas into practice.

Acknowledgments

I am indebted to a host of friends and colleagues who over the years have helped form this book in the deepest recesses of my brain:

Chris Mueller Sitze, selfless and loving soul mate.

Amy, Adam, and Aaron Sitze (and their families), who choose every day to live simply.

Present and former Evangelical Lutheran Church in America (ELCA) colleagues Tim Frakes, Marilyn Shomler, Ted Schroeder, Johanna Olson, Rachel Ronning Lindgren, Anita Chupp, Mark Burkhardt, Jon Skogen, Laurel Hensel, Sue Edison-Swift, Jenn Barger, Nancy Arnison, Kathy Sime, and Andy Waters for their example and encouragement when others thought that this wasn't an important part of my work.

Gerald Iversen, Mike Wilker, Rod Boriack, Jay Beech, Sally Simmel, Anne Basye, Lanny Westphal, Greg Kaufmann—the dreamers and schemers who plotted a possible simple-living emphasis for the ELCA during a cool fall weekend awhile back. Their thoughts fill the important nooks and crannies of this book.

Beth Gaede, word wizard and friend, whose editing on this our third book together came from her own passion and practice of this subject.

Andrea Lee, whose careful copyediting eyes kept my mistakes and imprecisions from your eyes.

All the simple lifestyle practitioners whom I have met over my years in the ELCA, whose passion for simplicity was as plain as the nose on their face and as magnificent as the fire in their eyes. Thankfully, your number is growing, as is your influence on the church!

~~~≈~~~

To those who know me, a confession: I've been watching you all these years. Listening under your words and looking at the movements of your eyes and hands. You may not have known it, but from watching you I have learned what's important and what's grace filled. Thanks.

~~~≈~~~

Introduction

～✃～

C an you imagine this?

    You are sitting there, thinking about how things are going in your church, and a rumpled-jeans-and-tan-work-shirt guy, with grey hair going in five directions, walks up to you and says, "I want to help you talk with people in your congregation about the way you all live." At first you are a little perplexed, because normally this kind of person doesn't approach you for no apparent reason. Normally, people you know well—much less people you have just met—don't talk about matters like this.

You catch the sparkle in the guy's eyes, though, and note that he doesn't seem too dangerous—no quivering, no sharp sticks, no tract-filled briefcase, no glasses held together with masking tape. So you decide to take him up on his offer, if only for a little while. You are a congregational leader, for goodness' sake, and you are interested in any conversation with the word *congregation* in it. You ask him to sit down, and the two of you start talking.

If you can imagine this scenario, you have also just imagined yourself into this book's content and approach. In the few short chapters here, you and I are going to think about starting heart-to-heart conversations in your congregation about simple living. This book is going to help you and others gather the courage and wisdom you need to live just and sustainable lifestyles that follow Jesus's commands and example.

꘎꘎꘎

So we should be satisfied just to have food and clothes.
—1 Timothy 6:8

꘎꘎꘎

One more thing to imagine: when you ask the guy why he wants to talk with you, he looks you straight in the eye and says, "It's time you did this, friend."

More about the Rumpled-Jeans Guy

If you think hard enough, this stranger could be one of many people you have encountered in your life. They are the people who appear at just the right moments in your life to lead you past large obstacles to some new stage or way of thinking. You bond almost instantaneously. You see into this person at the same time the person is peering into your soul. You engage in intense dialogue about what is really important to both of you. If you have stayed up all night at camp, fallen in love at first sight, traveled overseas, or met someone of another race or social class—then you may have had that experience. And when the conversation is over, both of you are changed—perhaps only in a small way—for the rest of your life.

I hope you and I can get to know each other better. I have met people like you and the people in your congregation and know enough about you that I want to have this conversation. Let me start by telling you more about me:

- I am a Lutheran Christian, radicalized in quiet ways by quiet teachers over the decades.
- My vocations in the church have included just about every manifestation of "church professional" you can imagine, except one: pastor. The list spans decades and includes

I'm descended from a combination of farm folks from the Ozarks and draft-dodging German nobility. I often think that these God-given genes and my heritages are the reason I'm both completely ordinary and completely extraordinary. I'm pretty sure that there's no contradiction between the two.

work in congregations and judicatories; wordsmithing; leadership roles with long titles; presenting and facilitating at conferences and retreats; and joyful attendance at meetings, of course.

- The best job I ever had: meat worker in South Lake Tahoe, California.
- I have been thinking about this "simple living" thing since I was a preteen.
- I am a teacher by trade and a learner by necessity.
- God's grace comes to me most visibly from my spouse and children.
- I think and work at the edges of ideas and organizations; someone once told me that is the place where living things do their growing.
- My strange hobbies: applying neurobiology to congregational dynamics and gathering firewood and twigs.

The rumpled-jeans? A real-life description of my preferred go-to-work uniform. We can talk about that if you like.

Instead, Let's Talk about Talking

Conversation—discourse, dialogue, banter, exchanges, talk, chatting—might be a better place to start than my workplace

~~≫≪~~

People love chopping wood. In this activity one immediately sees results.
—Attributed to Albert Einstein

~~≫≪~~

fashion. In one way, conversation is so simple as to defy description. Like a school of fish given a homework assignment to describe water, many people might have trouble trying to cobble together a useful definition of conversation. Their attempt would likely be peppered with, "Well, you know what I mean . . ." thus showing some frustration that they were asked to put into words something that, well, *everyone* already knows. All people converse, one way or another, and so may take for granted what is actually a very profound capacity of the human species.

Humans have this unique ability called language: words, symbols, and syntax that work together to enable thinking. Large human forebrains process language into mental maps that can be adapted and recalled for sharing with others. Words give people the facility to act, to remember ideas, to sort reality, to express self-awareness. In contemporary society's overlapping oral, magnetic, and written forms, people can carry words along with them—think cell phones, credit cards, or notepads—thus enabling folks to find and communicate meaning wherever they are, with whomever they meet.

Conversation changes bodies and brains. People engaged in heartfelt conversation intuitively find after only a few moments together a communication pattern or rhythm that fits the moment and the participants. Appreciative or loving conversation seems to reduce or disburse the brain's stress chemical, cortisol. During conversation, heart and respiration rates fall, as does blood pressure. Focused talking and listening require extensive coordination of brain functions—especially attention mechanisms—

~᠊ᠼ᠊~

*Talk with someone you trust about the first time you realized
that your way of living was way beyond your ability to sustain
it. How old were you? What brought you to think that way?
What happened next?*

~᠊ᠼ᠊~

and so conversation literally "takes our mind off" stressful
situations or feelings. Face-to-face communication enables facial
recognition—one function of a critical brain structure called the
amygdala, which governs much of the brain's response to danger
and the innate human capacity for social intelligence. With ges-
tures, odor recognition, and modulations of voice, individuals add
even more meaning to the sound patterns that they assemble as
words or sentences.

Unless people are sociopaths or truly devious, when they converse with someone else they are giving permission to be known by
that other person. In earnest conversations a person can come to
appreciate and trust another person. They slice through formali-
ties and boundaries and cut to the core of each other's true self.
In a world filled with lonely, busy people, the time and attention
given to a conversation can truly be a gift.

From my own experiences as a church leader, I can testify
how this happens. In my work, I necessarily spend a lot of time
on the phone with people from around the country. Every one of
those conversations—even the ones expressing criticism—makes
my day. When the phone goes back on its cradle, I am energized
by and grateful for the people I have just met. My mind is filled
with endorphins—the brain's feel-good chemical—and I feel really
privileged to have met yet another manifestation of God's Spirit
loose in the world. Every so often, I will meet someone in person
who remembers me from one of our conversations and expresses
almost exactly the same feeling about those moments!

Why Conversation Is a Method for Change

Because I know how conversations change us as individuals, I trust conversation as a method by which most important social changes take place. I am not alone in this opinion. Let me tell you about two people who have shaped my thinking in this matter.

Futurist and best-selling author Margaret Wheatley (*Turning to One Another: Simple Conversations to Restore Hope to the Future*) thinks of earnest conversation as the beginning of all social change. In her view, groups of people with ordinary shared interests—for example, eating, working, or playing—make decisions that coalesce as the foundation for social change.

I have experienced conversations like those Wheatley describes—in quiet moments before or after praying, on breaks at conferences, in times of verbal play and laughter, even seemingly silly events. I have learned that "conversation-as-method" rests on the principle from complexity theory that organisms can organize themselves or their environment with very few rules or outside influence. Complex at first sight, a conversation-based method of social change does not depend on management—for example, movement through an ordered agenda from established needs to possible solutions. Instead, the conversation takes on a life of its own—within an unpredictable context of circumstances and variables—and yields exciting ideas and energized decisions. When the conversation has run its course, some plan of action—if only taking one next step—emerges and the group makes implicit covenants to engage in those actions. Mutual accountability arises from the relationships among group members and grows strong because of the likelihood that the group will continue to talk together over time.

Where I work people seldom take coffee breaks but at lunch the conversations can range from the truly bizarre to the wildly hopeful. Sometimes the strangest comment will spark a colleague's creativity or a simple question will elicit an answer that blossoms

I've been deeply impressed by pastors who work in small, rural congregations. Most of these folks actually do read, pray, meditate, sit and think, know their members' daily work, and take sabbath time. Not that the rest of the pastors don't, of course.

into a new program or resource. Invitations to cooperate start with these lunch conversations—"Hey, sometime would you like to . . ."—as do the powerful forces of encouragement and forgiveness. Some folks walk together during their lunch hour, adding the benefits of physical activity to what others do while sitting together around tables.

You have probably seen something like these lunchtime conversations in your congregation. Think whether this has ever happened: At a quiet and relaxed moment, several people approach your pastor together and say, "So, Pastor, a few of us were talking and we thought that maybe . . ." Packed into that simple sentence stem are three valuable—and sometimes rare—ingredients for action or change in your congregation:

- Respectful or appreciative dialogue among people
- Decisions reached by consensus
- First action steps—finding someone else with whom to share the ideas

Wheatley also claims that deep conversation is an efficient method for change. Conversations move intuitively and quickly through topics and feelings; attention is focused; participants apply gentle persuasion without exciting large-scale resistance; moments of humor and forgiveness do their magic; most group members share their personal power fairly; participants offer their assets readily and they reach decisions more quickly than within formal planning or decision-making processes.

I remember visiting a congregation outside Hickory, North Carolina, where the pastor understood all this instinctively. He told me about a group of men—I will refrain from calling them "good old boys" because some folks might not understand the deep reverence that can come with this term—who sit out under a tree on Sunday mornings *during the pastor's Bible class.* The pastor respects these men for good reason, because he knows that years earlier their conversations under that tree kept the congregation alive during a difficult pastorate. He also knows that in their good-natured bantering and chatting, these men also deal with substantive matters regarding the congregation's vitality. What impressed me about the story was not only how weekly conversations were integral to this congregation's continuing health but also how this pastor was smart enough to value what these men were doing instead of attending his class.

Several years ago another visionary author, Frances Moore Lappé, wrote a book with her daughter Anna Lappé. After years of thinking and writing about the problems of world food distribution and consumption, the two women decided to find a hopeful counterpoint to the sad stories of hunger and injustice Frances had laid bare in her first book, *Diet for a Small Planet.* They set out on a journey to visit places in the world where social change was happening on a small-but-significant scale. In Brazil, India, Nicaragua and other widespread locations, the Lappés found a number of recurring patterns, including this one: small islands of social change were created and anchored by courageous people who talked together respectfully. In titling their book *Hope's Edge: The Next Diet for a Small Planet,* the two women were making a statement about the process of change: when people talk together, things change.

One effect of their book on me—during a time when I wrestled with the seeming hopelessness of the world situation—was that I wanted to find a few friends and head for a local coffee shop or the nearest pub to talk together until the waitstaff shooed us out of the place. Another reaction to the book: I would really like to put legs on an idea I heard about a few years ago. In the congregation I belong to, I would like to bring everyone together once a week during Advent around simple meals and cordial conversation in members' homes. Whoever showed up would be the right group and whatever they talked about would be the right topic.

What You Won't Find in This Book

Back to our conversation now. I want to be honest about what this book contains and doesn't contain. Here's what you won't find in this book:

1. This is not a book *about* simple living. Many marvelous works already exist, many of them classics—for example, *Small Is Beautiful* by E. F. Schumacher or *Voluntary Simplicity* by Duane Elgin. Although I will spend some time in chapter 2 giving you my personal take on the subject, you will find there only some of the most basic ideas that anchor the philosophy or practice of simplicity.

2. I am *not* going to help you figure out a plan for simplifying some part of your life. There is plenty of help out there for that necessary work—for example, *The Alternative Wedding Book* (published by Alternatives for Simple Living) or the classic *Living More With Less* by Doris Janzen Longacre.

3. You won't find this book chock-full of program ideas for your congregation to fit into existing structures or events. *Simple Living 101* (Alternatives for Simple Living) already does a good job with that task.

Why not those kinds of books? Please understand: each of the elements that I am *not* including in the book is important in its own right. But those kinds of books have already been written. So I have decided to focus on a single goal: Helping you start the conversation about simple living in your congregation.

What lies behind my logic? These three points:

1. *I am not sure that congregational programs are the place to start.* Many congregations are having a hard time holding together their formal structures and functions and an even harder time capturing the attention of most of their members. Because attention is the primary commodity for all human interaction—and thus absolutely necessary for groups of people trying to get anything done—I am going to help you with a necessary first step: to gather the willing attention of some members of your congregation around a subject of vital interest to them. The programs can follow later.

2. *After the first steps, you can figure out what to do next.* Once you start your conversations, and once they catch hold, you will be able to go to those other resources to find what you might need in addition to the considerable knowledge and skill you already possess.

3. *I would like to give you what you really want.* If I am right about how change happens, then you don't need more guilt, more creativity, or more ideas. What you probably want are more basic things like assurance that you are not weird for valuing a simple lifestyle; courage to approach others with questions and answers; hope that transcends whatever gets in its way, and forgiveness for the way you are living now. Those are the things I would like to talk with you about.

I've Not Always Thought This Way

For most of my professional career, I have cranked out enough programs and resources to fill a large portion of my resume and

⁓≋⁓

*As a staff member of a church body's national headquarters, I
often wonder whether the programs I invent and the resources
I produce add to or subtract from the basic simplicity of congregational life. Sometimes I feel guilty about not knowing
how to answer that question. Other times I keep inventing and
producing.*

⁓≋⁓

a large storage bin in my basement. My output over decades of
writing and leadership has targeted Sunday school, vacation Bible
school, intergenerational learning, youth ministry, stewardship,
evangelism, Christmas and Advent preparation, leadership development, adult faith formation, confirmation, hunger and justice,
worship, parenting, congregational planning, and even a salutary
workshop aimed at the neurobiological dimensions of a property
committee's ministries!

Irksome questions have lingered in my mind over the years,
however, as I have pounded or presented program ideas in paper
or pixels. The questions have included these:

- How can leaders know that "if the congregation builds
  it"—a fun congregational event, a cool curriculum with
  wowee-kazowee activities, a sermon with clever PowerPoint
  slides—"they will come"?
- Who, really, is paying attention to congregational leaders
  or congregational matters? Despite leaders' most fervent
  wishes or most plaintive bleatings, congregations are losing
  market share to marketers, time-at-church to time-at-soccer,
  and "God's money" to "my money."
- Why are congregational leaders trying to out-hustle hus-
  tlers, out-shout noisy people, or out-trick tricksters? Do we
  really think that deeper matters of the human spirit can be
  manipulated by methods that rely on bling, noise, sexual

innuendo, victory or glory, pleasure seeking, or becoming one of the popular kids?

- How do human brains process matters of integrity, life purpose, identity, or self-appreciation?
- Why do people always seem to try so hard at what seems so futile?
- What *would* Jesus do?

Up until recently, I have not really found good answers to these questions in most programs or resources. Working with the good folks at Alban Institute has strengthened my resolve to avoid placing too much trust in programmatic fixes for every congregational hiccup, however. From just a quick look at Alban's published books, I can see that I am in good company—along with you—when I look for new ways to think of congregational vitality rather than buy the latest surefire technique or acronym-laced program.

What This Book Will Include

Remember me as the rumpled-jeans guy at the start of this introduction? And what I first said to you in the imagined scenario? It went like this: "I want to help you talk with people in your congregation about the way you live." That is the heart and soul of this book in one sentence. But let me dress up the idea a little more.

This Book Is about You

Participants in an earnest conversation don't just talk about ideas. Eventually the questions—and their answers—get personal or even intimate. People are drawn to each other because they want to be known and to know others. So in this book, "simple living" is going to be about *your* lifestyle; "conversations" will mean *your* interaction with others and "actions" will be about what *you* might do within your congregation.

You Will Be Talking with Me

In this book I will raise some of the shades of my life so that you find encouragement to lead others towards simple living. My stories will not be about my great successes but about my own struggles to keep things simple, joyful, manageable. I don't expect that you will find me to be a paragon of simplicity—I don't own a bicycle or a hand-me-down push mower. Instead, think of me as someone still seeking deeper simplicity, gratitude, and servanthood.

You Will Talk with Yourself

Every so often as you read, you will want to put this book down, put on your prayer shawl, and do some seriously grateful thinking about your own life. Mostly about how you are probably already living more simply than you thought! If you keep a journal, that will be a good place to fill pages with some possibly new self-talk.

You Will Do Something with What You Read

I am going to challenge you to take action as you are reading. I will use strange and clever ways of helping you find strong and lasting reasons to do more than yammer about good ideas. Look for the places where I stop the conversation in its tracks and ask you to try something. I am sure you will be willing to accept the challenge.

You Will Discover Other Kernels of Change

Throughout the book you will find places where I have scattered seeds that you can plant in your own life or congregation. In some cases, they may look like marginal asides or simple questions. In other cases I will be upfront and tell you: "Look over here!" or "Let me tell you a story." Some of the seeds will germinate new ways of thinking and others will germinate new ways of behaving. Because I don't know the ground you will be tilling, it is up to

Live simply, so others may simply live.
—Attributed to Mahatma Gandhi

you to figure out how to get the seeds planted in the right place at the right time.

You Might Imagine Yourself into a Different Congregation

I have a vision—perhaps not fully formed—that small, flexibly organized congregations can be the primary place where people learn to live according to Christ's example. Many of the scores of congregations I have visited in my work and many of the scores of congregational leaders I have known have begun rethinking the purpose and nature of their work with this basic idea in mind: The church may be the only place where God's people are freed from the constraints of impossible lifestyles. In these pages you will see the vision for congregations that I share with these leaders.

You Will Become Part of an Imaginary Conversation Group

You will follow a group of people who have come together to engage this subject at the deepest core of their being. Reading about this imaginary circle of friends, you will have a chance to try on some of the possibilities that might emerge if you sat down with a group of folks from time to time to talk about life.

It's Time You Did This, Friend

You are living within a small window of time when widespread lifestyle change could actually have a lasting effect on the course

~✌~

In a survey of 37,000 recent college graduates, 59 percent listed as their top career goal balancing their personal and professional lives.
—*From the* Minneapolis Star Tribune, *April 18, 2007.*

~✌~

of the world's history. All around you, more and more people are coming to the realization that they just can't keep living this way. Many of the people you know are ready to reframe their thinking about life's most important questions. They are ready to talk with you.

By engaging others in heartfelt conversation, you can take advantage of this moment of God's own making. In a world seemingly gone mad with people rushing around, piling up senseless debt, frantic about being happy, and overloaded with brain-numbing information, you and others together can do the following:

- Find wisdom in the middle of life's sometimes messiness.
- Discover how to be satisfied with what you have.
- Turn down the volume on noisy temptations.
- Turn the spotlight on quiet temptations.
- Become even more generous with the time and money God provides you.
- Get over your addictions, especially the not-so-obvious ones.
- Help others remember who God is, what Christ did, how the Holy Spirit shows up in their lives.
- Consistently tell the truth and live with integrity.
- Confess, forgive, question, condemn, support, care, and affirm.
- Frame and maintain your sense of identity as a person set apart for God's purposes.

- Find Christ in other people, other places, other situations.
- Help congregation members hold their marriages or families together.

Stop for a Moment

Don't move to the next chapter quite yet. Before you go any further, flip back through this chapter's pages and circle the phrases or sentences that most accurately reflect the personal yearnings that brought you to this book in the first place. (Hint: don't forget to read the top-margin notes.) Now go back and look at what you have circled. What patterns do you see—repetitions, contradictions, or trains of thought—and what do they suggest about you? Finally, take time to pray—with yourself or someone who knows you—about the ways God has led you to this way of thinking.

1

How's It Going, Really?

≈≈≈

The worship service ends. Scores of worshipers dutifully head out of the sanctuary toward the exit doors, where they will greet the preacher with a polite, squishy handshake and then make a beeline for either the donuts or the front door.

Between "Go in peace and feed the hungry. Amen" and "Nice sermon, Pastor" are some awkward moments of semiconversation. They are familiar little pieces of politeness that fill the silence and get people out of the church before they have to ask or say anything important. It's a hard thing, but most folks manage to shuffle their way to the pastor's handshake without saying much at all to anyone about anything.

Some folks—yes, I am one of them—absolutely thrill at the challenge of making these few seconds into something useful: welcoming a visiting family, checking on a long-absent worshiper now returned, joshing with the wonderful "little old ladies" who are usually *not* little or old inside their heads. And I never do church committee business during these walking-and-talking times.

Short as they are, these are the moments I use quick and appreciative questions to let folks know that I care about them and their lives. Instead of the obligatory, sometimes empty "How are you?" my curious queries go something like this:

- What's coming up this week?
- How are things working out for you these days?

Collect and practice using some new and thoughtful responses to the standard "Hi, how are you?" greeting. Think how simplicity could be part of that short response. One example: "Happy to be alive."

- You still working at the same job?

What I get out of those kinds of questions is far different than "Fine, and how are you?" In just a few sentences I can usually find out what is *really* happening in folks' lives. More important, I can honor them for who they really are.

Sometimes the conversations end up with no more than a blessing for the week or an assurance of prayer. Other times I stick around and finish what the question started. (As I am writing this, I am helping a guy in our church find another job after his business partner shut him out of his own office.) Sometimes, a few exchanged sentences at a time, these chats extend for several weeks or even months. In every case, the conversations are worth the time and effort it takes to put away my natural Lutheran shyness and approach someone with more than cultured courtesy.

Walking Out of Church with You

Right now, at the start of this book, you and I are walking out of church together, and I want to know how you are, how things are really going. For as long as it takes to read this book, you and I are going to have a conversation about you and your congregation. My questions are similar to those we might have if we were shuffling towards the pastor after worship, but with a purpose just slightly more focused. I really want to know:

*One of the things I have noticed in visiting congregations
around the country: some are really junky and cluttered, and
others are neat and organized. I have wondered how each kind
of congregation got to be that way.*

- What's at the center of your congregation?
- If you are a pastor (or other leader), how close are you to the end of your rope?
- What's it taking out of your hide to keep this congregation moving or afloat?
- What would it take for you to try something new—really new—or something important—really important?
- How do you decide what is really important in life, and what isn't?

If you and I could talk about those questions together, we would learn a lot about each other, and in a few moments get to what's at the center of our hearts and minds.

If You Had Asked Me a Few Years Ago

If you had asked me any of those questions a few years ago—when I was hip deep in the workings of the congregations I served—I would have given you answers that you might expect:

- Christian education is at the heart of our church. We do "faith formation" really well here, and I would love to involve you in our new efforts at intergenerational learning experiences.

- Stewardship is what makes us tick around here. We understand what stewardship is all about, and you can see it in the way we attract and hold volunteers like you.
- The end of my rope? I hate to admit it, but the rope is sliding out from under my grip and my fingers are getting rope burn. I would love to talk with you more if you have the time.
- I am working too hard, too long, and with too much on my plate. Know the feeling?
- Sure, I'm interested in "new"—always have been and always will be—but I have to tell you right away that I'm not a sucker for razzmatazz or hustles. Now, what do you have in mind?
- What's important? Right now all of it is important. Why do you ask?

You can see that I would answer perhaps much like you. Like you, I have been a hard-working, loyal, brave, and courageous congregational leader. Like you, I have been filled with strong resolve to keep using whatever plow God has stuck into my hands to get done well what needed to be done. What you might not see, though, is that my answers wouldn't have really satisfied me back then. Probably not the people who asked the questions, either.

If You Asked Me the Same Questions Now

My answers would be different now. Over the past few years I have noticed something in my service in various congregational ministries—where my heart will always be—and I would like to describe that nagging notion. (Think of my description here both as a question—"You ever feel this way?"—and as my honest feeling about church.) What I have noticed is that I am not as content to plug away at things that don't really make a difference in the lives of the people of the congregation. It may be disloyal

~~><~~

Once when I worked in a congregation, at budget-approval
time I surprised the voters at the meeting by inviting them to
reveal their own levels of income, their pension plans, and their
perks in the same way they were publicly dissecting my salary
and benefits. No one accepted my invitation.

~~><~~

or even nonsensical, but my test for the good that comes from congregations starts with a single question: what difference will this program, resource, event, presentation make in the daily lives of the members?

If I can't get an emotionally or intellectually honest answer (or if the question gets turned around, as in "But what about the difference this program, resource, event, presentation will make in the congregation's mission?"), I am just not as interested anymore. No, I'm not tired. No, I'm not cynical. Something else is going on here.

What I have come to realize is that for all these years of service in the church—I'm at about 40 years now and counting—I have wished for evidence of some rock-solid centers to congregational identity and purpose that I could say were really biblical, really important, really central to the stewardship of life to which Christians are called. Some core benefit that I don't have to smear all over God's people like spiritual makeup. Some idea I don't have to force-feed them. Some truths I don't have to pretend are important. Some big rocks that I don't have to keep pushing uphill. Some lifework that attracts men as well as women. Some good news that connects with people's real yearnings and matches their innate capacities.

You have already read this far, so you already know my answer to those yearnings. I think congregations could be places whose central identity went something like this: we are the folks who help you live a just, manageable, and sustainable life.

～✺～

*The more I study brain science the more I'm sure that "too much"
and "too fast" don't exactly sit well with most brains. Some days
I wonder what will happen when all of our brains become so
confused that most of us won't be satisfied about anything or
anyone. And then what?*

～✺～

Outside the Church Doors

If you and I had taken that Sunday morning walk out of church
and kept going—back home or to work the next day—we would
eventually have encountered the rest of the worlds in which we
live. Since most of "lifestyle" happens outside of churches, let's
take an honest look at the condition of the world in which your
simple living will take place.

How's it going, really, in the world around you? Try these
questions and some of my answers.

How Much Longer Can Things Keep Going on This Way?

The results of humanity's increasingly materialistic lifestyles are
sucking the life out of this planet and its people and other living
things more quickly than ever before and perhaps irrevocably.
Not much more time remains—less than a decade by some
accounts—before slight downward trends become sliding spirals.

Who Benefits from Your Way of Living?

Someone at the end of some economic power equation is probably profiting greatly from your lifestyle decisions. They may not
always have in mind your long-term well-being.

With other people, survey current advertisements in magazines or newspapers, looking for evidence of a general societal yearning for just, sustainable, or manageable lifestyles. Talk about what you find, especially how it might affect your congregation.

What's Broken and Not Getting Fixed?

The number of people in the world who are living on less than two dollars a day is increasing. The availability of clean water and air is decreasing. Forests are disappearing. Fear between nations and their peoples is increasing while international security is decreasing. Credit-card debt, mortgage foreclosures, and bankruptcies are trending upward. Visible and invisible wars are being waged all around us.

Who Is Voluntarily Downshifting or Downsizing?

An increasing number of families are choosing to reduce their consumption of goods and the planet's resources, to bring their schedules under control, and to concentrate on what's truly important in life. All around you may be people who are living simply, perhaps invisibly so.

Who's Being Mature?

An increasing number of corporations and decision-making bodies in the world understand that as grownups they need to think about the long haul. Some business and government leaders are giving up on shortsighted views of the bottom line. These folks could be your allies or your teachers.

Where Do You Find Wisdom in the Face of Turmoil?

In spite of the problems that threaten your vision of a godly lifestyle, you probably know people who seem serenely confident and joyful. They are curiously attractive to your spirit and perhaps good examples of how you could live and think.

Stop for a Moment

This is a good place to do something with what you have read. Try charting onto paper a "mind map" of your perceptions or feelings about the state of the worlds in which you live:

- Give names to at least five of your thoughts—for example, "Fed up" or "Getting Better"—and draw boxes around them.
- With arrows and dotted lines, connect the named-and-boxed thoughts to your answers to questions like: What's acceptable about the world situation? Unacceptable? What's working? Who or what gives you hope? What in your lifestyle is just about ready to break?
- When you have constructed a fairly complete map—or run out of time—look at what you have captured in this diagram of thoughts and look for patterns that tell you something about your prevalent mood or framework for approaching life.

꩜

Owning a lot of things won't make your life safe.
—*Luke 12:15*

꩜

Back to You

Let's come back to you and your situation. Because you have picked up this book and because you have read at least this far, I am going to presume that these things are true about you:

Some Kind of Simple Living Is Important to You

You have thought about it a lot; you are trying to live that way and you are wondering how to keep at this kind of stewardship in spite of everything else going on inside of you and outside of you.

You Are Not Completely Sure What Simple Living Is All About

You are smart enough to have hunches about the subject—it's about cutting back on what's not necessary—but are hoping there is more to it than giving up life as you know it. You have never wanted to be a recluse or an eccentric, so you are looking for a lifestyle characterized by something more than "No."

You Have Some Doubts about Whether Simplicity Really Works

You have studied basic economics, know about goods, services, and consumption. You know how money flows between buyers and sellers; you make your living in a world of rewarded competitiveness. Deep down you wonder what would happen if everyone lived this way. Your questions are smart and well-intentioned.

❦

Amount by which Americans' total spending in 2005 exceeded their earnings: $41.6 billion.
—*U.S. Bureau of Economic Analysis, reported in "Harper's Index,"* Harper's Magazine, *April 2006.*

❦

You Look at the World around You . . .

You look at the world around you and realize that not much time may be left before the planet gets really sick, people start getting really selfish and fearful, the economy really starts crumbling, or all of us start really paying for the way some of us live.

You Are a Leader

Perhaps you are a pastor or other professional church worker. Maybe you are part of the congregation's inner circle of hard-working, loyal, trustworthy, and brave leaders. Or maybe you are just someone who has found that other people ask you important questions and listen when you answer. People pay attention to you.

You Are Searching

Perhaps you are searching for something different or new. You still have whole drawers full of magic bullets—file folders filled with notes and notebooks from conferences, retreats, and discipleship festivals—and bookshelves stacked to the ceiling with really good books that you have read. But you wonder if you need to know or ask something more.

You Feel Alone

You are alone, if only in your own estimation. Welcome to the crowd; most leaders I know are more than just a little bit lonely

〜✦〜

The few simple-living people I know are oddballs in so many ways. They're the kind of folks who waltz when the different drummers come along. I'm the same kind of person, although I don't dance, on account of my strict upbringing. Still, the waltzers and I get along.

〜✦〜

down deep. It may come with the territory, but it doesn't feel good to be out there in front of the folks you lead—or to the side of them or noticeably different from them. You probably know what it feels like to leave a late-night meeting convinced that no one understood more than 10 percent of what you were talking about. When it comes to living simply, you may *really* feel alone when you look around at the way other folks seem to be living their lives.

You Feel Called to Help Other Folks

You feel called to helping the ones who want to change their ways of approaching life. You are not nosey or pushy, but you know that many other congregation members are just barely hanging on to what they call "a good life." You think that if they and you could just talk, perhaps together you could find a way out of consumptive, wasted, fruitless, and frantic ways of living.

You Know How People Change

You know that yet another program, another thrilling speaker, another self-help manual, or another series of six classes probably isn't going to change much at all. You see the implicit contradiction in inventing a complex and difficult-to-maintain program to help people live simply.

Am I getting close here? See yourself in this mirror? Does the photograph resemble you?

⟋⟍

Purpose-greed—a mental or spiritual affliction felt primarily by those who are overmotivated to "make a difference in the world." Sometimes prevalent among church leaders. Synonym: "change agency."

⟋⟍

You Look Like Someone I Know

I know people whose photographs look like you. They live where I live—in a comfortable, mostly Christian suburb of Chicago. Others meet in simplicity circles in the city. These people include folks who buy fresh produce from vegetable co-ops in the Bay Area, back-to-the-land people in the Sierras, prairie poets and shepherds in the Dakotas, retired women and men who have moved back to small towns in the South, sustainable agriculture advocates in New England, and cultural critics in the Pacific Northwest—all of them holding tightly to the same ideals you do.

Some of them write powerfully about their experiences, some organize poor people into cooperatives, others run food pantries or community gardens, and still others bring large groups of people together in quiet retreat settings. Some even work in congregations. Some of them are my admired friends; most of them give me courage or teach me. One of them is my spouse, three of them my adult children, two of them my mother and (now deceased) father.

Like you, they tend to be quiet folks, by definition not the kind of people you would notice right away. Because they don't make headlines—"Crazed Vegetable Advocates Attack Local Meat Market"—they may be as unobtrusive as a zucchini squash hiding in a garden.

When they are people of faith—the kind of people who might be part of your congregation—they are sometimes disappointed

Send or say "Thank you!" to seven people today. Be genuine, be specific, be ready for what happens next.

with some of what they see in the church as an enterprise. They may see church leaders rushing around trying to accomplish too many worthy goals, pushing for "more" or "bigger." These simplicity seekers watch their self-satisfied congregations leading satiated lives that show little regard for the wider world. These simple-living folks may also be aware of how sadly unmanageable their congregations have become and may feel sorry for leaders of that kind of faith community.

Like you, though, they still have hope for their congregations.

Back to Your Congregation

Let me try to describe the general context in which I think you find spiritual sustenance, the place where you might be putting this book to work. Your congregation may look like this:

It's a Group of Basically Good People

Some people in your congregation may be slightly loopy when they get onto some subjects, but they are still basically good-hearted. You know enough of them by name and by circumstance that you can call them friends. You would like to know a lot more of them as friends.

The 80-20 Rule Is Alive and Well

About 20 percent of the people do about 80 percent of the work. They keep the place running, perhaps not as well as you would like it to work. Your church used to function better, but for a few years now it's been hard to find qualified and eager volunteers to serve on committees, task forces, and governing bodies. The committees and teams limp by for now.

Women Are Prominent

Women are behind most of what's good about your congregation. Increasingly they are the ones who make—and carry out—major decisions. They are insistent, they are intuitive, and they are interesting. Both men and women pay attention to them.

Your Pastor Is Running at Full Capacity All the Time

Your pastor functions basically as the major glue holding the congregation together. Your congregation is known by the qualities of your pastor. That's not bad because your pastor seems to be content with that role. ("Your pastor" might be you.)

People Seek New Directions

Some people—the pastor included—get what being a Christian means. From their comments, their activity and inactivity, maybe even their looks, you sense that they are itching to take the congregation in a different direction, but are holding back for now. These folks fascinate you and maybe frighten you a little, too.

Your Congregation Does the Basic Things

Like most congregations, yours covers the basics—Sunday school, a hunger offering every now and then, regular worship services, an okay choir, some attempts at fellowship and service, maintenance of the property, and paying the bills. A few people push for additional good things to do and are willing to carry the ball and pay the freight to realize their passions.

─∾≺∾─

*Let the same mind be in you that was in Christ Jesus, who,
though he was in the form of God, did not regard equality with
God as something to be exploited, but emptied himself, taking
the form of a slave, being born in human likeness.*

—Philippians 2:5-7 NRSV

─∾≺∾─

Your Congregation Has Its Share of Marginal Members

In the background of your congregation are lots of marginal
members, folks who you know about but don't know that well.
They come to worship enough times not to be considered "inac-
tives," but they rarely participate in the congregation's programs
or events. They are good people, too—you know about them
from the positive influence they have in your community—but
for some reason they just don't connect all that much with your
congregation.

Some Folks Are Living at Some Edge or Another

People are working too many jobs, facing too many personal
problems, chasing too many activities for their children, living
from one paycheck to another. Every so often one of them will slip
away from your congregation for a while, but they still consider
themselves as members. Sometimes you wonder whether they think
that church is the place where they go only if everything else is
going okay in their lives. "Doing okay" is getting harder, though,
for more and more people.

People Are Looking for Real Community

Many members harbor the unspoken wish that they could get to
know each other better. Not at a superficial level but as real people

❧❧

During the 2004–2005 biennium, consumer nonmortgage debt increased 12.5 percent, settling to an average of $11,669 early in 2006.

—From Experian Consumer Direct, reported in the Chicago Tribune Magazine, *October 15, 2006.*

❧❧

with important things to say to each other, important things to know and do together.

Simple Living Is Not Part of the Program

"Simple living" is probably nowhere on the playlist of your congregation's iPods. You can't find this theme anywhere in the congregation's structure; you have not seen any mention of this topic in the congregation's mission statement, and you don't hear much about this subject in newsletters or sermons.

Sound like the place you hang your hat on Sundays, where you roll up your sleeves to work? How does this photograph compare with the one of yourself?

The Pictures Can Merge

I have been part of eleven congregations in my adult life, all over this country. Eleven groups of God's people gathering for purposes beyond themselves. Eleven sets of leaders—usually my friends or colleagues—and eleven vision and mission statements. Some of them were ordinary congregations, although one or two marched to really different drummers. I have also lived in two nontraditional faith communities, less formal manifestations of the body of Christ.

During the early years of our marriage, Chris and I avoided accumulating lots of stuff by moving every few years or so. Now that we have lived in this house for almost 20 years, the basement is filling up. Maybe it's time to move again.

In only one of these groups—almost 30 years ago—did I ever experience any emphasis in simple living or lifestyle stewardship (another way to describe this matter theologically). It was a very nice class that lasted a very short six weeks. I was sad when it finished because we had just gotten to the point where we were talking honestly—"How many pairs of shoes do you own, Bob?"—and then we all went our separate ways. (Back then I owned only three pairs of well-worn shoes; now I am up to five, two of them less than a year old.)

That's probably when I realized that a way to merge the two photographs had to be possible—the one showing people like you yearning to find others like yourself and the other photo depicting congregations like yours yearning to find a central purpose that connects with most of its members. Back then I saw a glimmer of what might happen if like-minded people in a congregation started a conversation about what really matters. I imagined what would occur if we spent another six weeks together, changing the questions and listening to each other more intently.

I thought then as I think this very moment: Congregations are the perfect place to bring together people who need purposes with purposes that need people. Life in Christ meeting life in the world. The wisdom of God's Spirit filling up the empty places in people's souls. People filling empty pews because they are getting what they need to make sense out what seems utterly senseless in the way they live.

*While he was still alive, I called my elderly father long dis-
tance every night. I always asked, "What've you been doing?"
For years his answer was always, "Sitting here contemplat-
ing my good fortune." Right before he died, he was legally
blind, suffering from gathering dementia, and not quite
sure about lots of things. I'm sure, though, that "God-blessed"
still described his life.*

How's It Going, Really?

I am always surprised when I ask that question—even with strangers. One time I asked this question of a colleague who doesn't like
to talk about herself. The look I got first told me: don't mess with
my head. But when this woman let the word *really* soak in, that
idea became like the latch on a window that just got opened to
let in a little fresh air. She started talking about what was and was
not so good in her life. Eventually she asked me the same question back, and I opened the shades on my windows. That was a
good conversation.

The same thing might happen if you and I were to talk about
the same question. So let's go back to the original query that
framed this chapter's beginning thoughts: how is it going, really,
with you, your worlds and your congregation? (Or maybe how
would you like it to be going?)

If your answers are—or have been—framed in less-than-
satisfactory terms or if you have found yourself pretty accurately
described in my photographs, then we have a place to start together. (If not, you can keep reading, of course!)

*Call a friend who taught you something valuable about being
satisfied. Take as much time as you need to thank this person.
Be sure you explain why you're grateful.*

Starting in a Good Place

Where we can start is definitely *not* in a position of destitution, like
a pine forest in a drought. In fact, I see you as superbly capable,
a walking and talking shopping cart of wonderful assets. If the
photographs match your situation right now, I think of you as eminently equipped to begin working within your congregation—in
a nonprogrammatic way—to make simple living important to the
people you know and love there. In other words, what looks like
a pile of problems—"We're floundering in ordinariness, we don't
know where we're going, we're a bunch of blah people, we aren't
growing"—is in fact a good starting place for people who want to
make their congregations into places that are simply centered.

Here's why:

1. Once you have bottomed out—on lifting yourself up by
    your own bootstraps, on thinking of yourself more highly
    than you ought, on flailing about for rescue from someone
    else—then you are ready to head back up. From my own
    experience I know what all swimmers know: you can float
    better if you stop thrashing around in the water.

2. You haven't lost your yearning for depth, importance, core
    elements of church. Way down deep, you haven't gotten
    tired—about Christ or his calling in your life. Way down
    deep, you haven't gotten cynical—you still love God's
    people and the world.

3. You know what you are good at doing, what you like to do, what it means to call in favors, what the shape and direction of your personal influence is.
4. You are ready for the power of honest, emotional conversation as the central element by which all important changes happen.
5. You are ready to try what few have done before you, to be quietly different, to engage strangers and friends in another way of thinking about church.

By the way, in some circles you would be described as "asset rich," and a map of your capabilities would fill walls with delightful, useful gifts of God. I have helped people assemble scores of these maps, and every one of them usually includes a set of assets that would have otherwise been labeled "Our Problems." These folks are usually embarrassed that they didn't see capabilities living inside presumed deficits.

~~❦~~

Stop for a Moment

Whatever your mood right now, take some time to make a little map of your God-given assets—gifts that are useful. With some Post-it notes and markers in hand, write down specific answers to the following questions, one answer per Post-it. These will be some of your assets. The questions:

- What are you good at doing?
- What were you good at doing in the past?
- What do you like to do?
- Who do you know (that owes you)?
- What do you have that's useful?

Look at your written assets and see if they help you know how you might begin conversations. Arrange them in clusters of related ideas and possibilities. See what these maps tell you about yourself.

Moving On

This chapter has meandered through my imagined conversation with you. About yourself, your church, your feelings about both. We have looked at some photographs together, and we have figured out that you are ready for the rest of the book. As you continue to turn pages—and read them, of course!—you will start to see how this continuing conversation becomes a gentle process of encouraging you to begin leading your congregation toward simplicity as one of its core convictions, its core identities, and its core behaviors.

Whoso loves
Believes the impossible.
—Elizabeth Barrett Browning

2

Simplicity Itself

~~~≈✦≈~~~

B efore we start the conversation about *your* conversations, we need to explore the idea of simplicity itself, especially as a theological concept and spiritual practice. If you poked around in a dictionary or thesaurus, you would find simplicity described in the following ways:

- the property, condition, or quality of being simple or un-combined
- the absence of luxury or showiness
- plainness
- the absence of affectation or pretense
- the lack of sophistication or subtlety
- naivete
- a lack of good sense or intelligence
- foolishness
- clarity of expression or austerity in embellishment

Notice how most of these definitions are about deficits, scarcity, or other insufficiency? By these descriptions it would seem that simplicity is known by what you don't have or don't experience.

In my own lexicon, simplicity itself is rooted in theology and is lived out as a spiritual practice. In this way of thinking, simple living is characterized by abundance, capacity, and possibility. In this chapter, we will see how those ideas make simplicity a matter of grateful, joyful living.

~~≈~~

Stop for a Moment

Compare these definitions with your thoughts about simple living. How could you turn around deficit-laden dictionary definitions to describe more abundant, joyful living? On a small piece of paper write new definitions or synonyms for *simplicity* or *simple living*. Fold the page into a bookmark reminder as you read the rest of this book.

~~≈~~

Simplicity Systematics

When it comes to systematics—that is, doctrinal formulations nicely arranged in an attractive framework—simple living is part of stewardship, itself part of what Christians refer to as "the sanctified life." Let's look at some of the places where simplicity fits into the framework of beliefs within the Christian tradition, tenets of a "simplicity theology" that might connect with your own understanding of doctrine.

Your Life Is Not Your Own

God created—but didn't give away—the world and everything in it. Jesus redeemed—but didn't excuse—you from sin's effects. The Spirit emptied—but didn't waste—God's bounty of gifts on you and the rest of God's people. A theology of simple living starts with the proposition that everything you have, every ability you name, and every relationship that comes your way—all equip you for your

～✦～

Simplicity is the ultimate sophistication.
—Attributed to Leonardo da Vinci

～✦～

primary role in life: to praise and serve God and the people God has always loved. This is much simpler than trying to praise and serve yourself and the people you hope will always love you.

God's Grace Works

Grace lubricates caring human relationships. Grace nourishes starved souls looking for purpose and meaning. Grace protects you from having to prove your worth by amassing piles of possessions or engaging in frenzied multitasking. God's undeserved favor becomes tangible in the grace shown by God's people.

I can attest to the power of God's grace. I grew up with a strong sense of inferiority. A skinny, gawky kid, I didn't get to one hundred pounds until I was a senior in high school. No parties, no real girlfriends, no dating in high school. I played the pipe organ for endless hours and would have been content to remain a talented-but-shy church musician. Down deep, though, I believed that I didn't possess most of what I needed to be who I really wanted to be: a leader in the church. My tearful private prayers in high school usually started with the weight of my inferiority. (In case you don't know, inferiority feelings are unmanageable and horribly complex, thus not part of simple living.)

During the first week of college, God's grace showed up in the form of some wild-and-crazy classmates who decided to make me their project. A kind of geek makeover, I think, or like dressing up a pig. They saw in me other gifts from God that had lain dormant all those years: My sense of humor, my listening ear, my intuitive sense of others' needs, my ability to rally people to a

~~✦~~

*We didn't bring anything into this world, and we won't take
anything with us when we leave.*
—*1 Timothy 6:7*

~~✦~~

cause, my talent for carving language into new shapes. Over time
they invested in our friendship, giving me chances to join them
as leaders and insisting that I stifle the inferiority feelings enough
to become the person God had already formed. They taught me
to have fun. Without the blessing of these now-lifelong friends,
my life would have been a tangle of complicated efforts to prove
myself as more than my imagined inferiorities. I know that grace
works because God's grace in these classmates turned Bob the
Beggar into Bob the Builder.

God's Grace Is Sufficient

Enough is a theological word, especially in the face of real or
imagined needs or difficulties. God takes the first steps—creating,
redeeming, making you holy. God provides, sometimes strangely,
sometimes not on your timetable, but always enough. Because you
deserve nothing, God's enough is always a gracious gift. When
you wake up to your undeservedness, you understand that you
are abundantly blessed by a loving and gracious God. And you
are satisfied. Now you can get through life happy to have enough
to get through life.

Stewardship Is How You Respond to God's Grace

Stewards like you carry out the will of the Owner, even when the
Owner has offered only a few guiding principles and even when
the Owner seems to be gone. The Owner has a gracious and loving plan—in New Testament Greek, an *economia*—that reaches

~~~

Steward—someone who knows and carries out the plan of the owner. It's been said that the steward was the sty-warden, the serf at the bottom of the castle in the mud and muck, working with the pigs. Styg-waerden became sty-warden became steward. In contemporary life, a feedlot operator. In contemporary theology, a mature disciple who does more than follow the household rules.

~~~

from the past to redeem the future. As a steward (*economos*), you carry out your part of God's plan every day of your life. You choose your work within that overall plan, not burdened by the weight of a micromanaging Owner or worried that you will break the household rules. One part of the plan: that the world's riches would remain sustainable over generations.

Simple Living Brings Deep and Lasting Joy

Through the Holy Spirit's work, God makes it possible for you to live a full and pleasurable life, brimming over with gratitude to God and love for the whole world. Because you are a steward of God's will, you can sidestep the endless circles of self-centeredness that eventually bury deep joy under mounds of trivial happiness. Living simply, you serve God unencumbered by the excessive weight of a rushed and possession-heavy life. At a biological level, when your brain is living simply, it's not choked with the toxins of stress chemicals; it's more easily delighted, more capable of pleasing connections with God and with other people.

The Church Exists for the Benefit of the World

The church gathers and calls saved and gifted people in order to get God's work done in the world God so dearly loves. The world beyond your front door needs to hear gospel—good news. But

❧

The Self-Storage Association reported in 2006 that its estimate of the number of self-storage facilities scattered across the country is at least 55,000, double the number of facilities just ten years earlier.

❧

beyond and after gospel proclamation through telling, there is gospel proclamation through living. Read the Bible carefully and you see that freeing the captives, binding up the brokenhearted, healing the sick, visiting those imprisoned, caring for widows and orphans—these actions are also framed as "good news."

At this moment in history, the world God loves is groaning under the weight of injustice and slowly being robbed of its capacity to sustain life. All around you, the people God loves are increasingly burdened by lifestyles they can't keep up for very much longer. You and your congregation are called to help turn that around.

Selfishness Is Its Own Reward and Punishment

Lifestyles crammed to the top with stuff and whirling at breakneck speed towards "happiness" certainly seem rewarding at first. Self-idolatry is the heart and soul of materialistic views of the "good life." Because selfishness automatically rewards itself, it may seem that selfishness can't be argued with.

But over time, Jesus warns, the rewards of selfishness are eclipsed by the costs. In the end, bigger barns don't save your soul. You reap the natural consequences of profligate living when you have nothing left to put into the barns; when you live in a lonely landscape devoid of true friends; when you wear down your body and brain with incessant seeking and holding. From stories of hoarded manna to the account of the rich young ruler,

Imagine yourself hovering above the entire congregation at worship, looking at all these wonderful people. As you look around, think who might fit any part of your description of someone who lives simply. Now imagine this group together at dinner some evening, talking about their yearnings for a more manageable or godly way to live. What fun!

the witness of Scripture is clear: your [good] life does not consist of the things you possess.

You Are Gathered into a Purposed Community of Faith

Being surrounded by all the rest of us provides something comforting for you. Left alone, you could fall prey to self-centeredness. Wrapped into the communion of saints by the Comforter, however, you direct your life outward, beyond yourself. Simplicity is one way of summarizing some of the basic tenets of the faith that you confess to others in the creeds of your faith community. You are instructed in consecrated living in the Lord's Prayer ("Give us our food for today" [Matt. 6:11]); the Ten Commandments ("Do not want anything that belongs to someone else" [Ex. 20:17].) and the Great Commandment ("You must love each other, just as I have loved you" [John 13:34]). The church holds you accountable to God's claim on your life. A young bachelor colleague of mine remarks that knowing whether he has any niggling faults—slurping soup or snoring—is hard because he has no one to tell him what's bothersome. Earnest and heartfelt conversation—including confession and forgiveness—ameliorates the emptiness of a self-centered lifestyle. Self-centered living is never simple. Simplicity becomes more possible when you live in purposed community.

*Whatever you say or do should be done in the name of the Lord
Jesus, as you give thanks to God the Father because of him.*
—*Colossians 3:17*

It's All about Jesus

In bringing simple lifestyles to the center of your faith-filled conversations, think of Jesus's own lifestyle, the things he said and
did. The things he didn't do. Consider the fact that the human
Jesus also woke up in the morning, yawned, scratched his beard,
had a cup of fair-trade coffee, and tried to make sense out of his
e-mails.

In concentrating only on Jesus-as-God, you may miss the fact
that the very human Jesus chose a lifestyle that fit the mission he
received at his baptism. The healer and preacher also had to think
about his next meal, his friendships, his enemies. He faced danger,
he laughed, he sat around and talked with folks. He walked everywhere he wanted to go. He criticized religious authorities and the
government, and he listened to farmers. He went to big dinners
with very important people. He observed spiritual practices but
didn't spend lots of time at his local synagogue. The point here
is not only that Jesus was human but also that in his lifestyle and
career choices—yes, he made them just like you do—Jesus chose
to live simply and joyfully in service to others.

Jesus's ministry was primarily directed at people suffering from
poverty and economic injustice. Theologians for centuries have
talked about seeing Jesus in the eyes of the poor. In these latter
days, neurobiologists now understand that face recognition—an
intelligence you were born with—is the primary means by which
you come to know others, to find your personal identity and to

know what to do. If you have the courage to come to know the faces of people who are poor, you have the chance to learn how to live simply, generously, joyfully—like Jesus.

~≈~

Stop for a Moment

From your personal or congregational collection of art, assemble a few drawings, paintings, or sculptures that show Jesus's face close up. Include some created by contemporary artists. Look at each one very carefully, especially at Jesus's eyes. What are the artists trying to say about Jesus by their portrayal of his eyes? What do you notice? How long can you stare without averting your eyes? What do the visual renderings stir in your soul? If you could talk to the Jesus portrayed in any of these works, what would be the first thing you'd say or ask him about your way of life? Which one of these depictions of Jesus might most inspire your daily living?

~≈~

At the Heart of Simple Living

Just in case you can't carry around in your head all the theological bases for simple living, here's the easiest way to describe the kind of simplicity I think we are called to live. One sentence, so you can remember: you know you are living simply when "enough" guides your decisions and when you know the difference between "yes" and "no." Too philosophical? Let me tell you about two of the dogs my wife and I have served over the years. (You have dogs or cats? Then you know that they are in charge and that you

～ゞゝ～

Carry in your pocket or purse a smooth touchstone that you've named "Enough."

～ゞゝ～

serve their needs, right?) Let's call them Greta and Crumpet and let's say that they had two very different approaches to "enough." Crumpet believed that food was to be eaten in its entirety anytime it appeared. Crumpet approached any offering of dog rations as an opportunity to gobble as much as possible in as short a time as possible. On the other hand, Greta would approach her dog dish with reverence, select a single morsel, and carry it gingerly to another location that was suitable for chewing and swallowing. Greta—the favored dog in this story—sometimes took hours to finish the proffered nuggets of food.

For Crumpet, the appearance of dog-groceries in her line of sight and smell was the major cause to gobble up every morsel as quickly as possible. Greta's more subdued "yes" still resulted in the satisfaction of her appetite, but was a more measured—thoughtful—approach. Like most dogs and some people, Crumpet confused "enough" and "yes" with "right now." Down deep in Greta's doggie brain—neurobiologists now think that animals might have emotions—she was content with what she had for that moment, trustful of the abundance that regularly appeared in that dog dish, and assured that her serving stewards—Chris and me—would care for her. Those two beloved dogs helped me years ago to give voice and action to "enough" as a joyful way of living.

Stephen Covey, the "effective living" guru, talks about the relationship of "yes" and "no," especially in the management of time. One concept from his books and training course has stayed with me for more than a decade: saying "no" to something is easier when a deeper "yes" burns inside of you. With this insight, Covey names simple living to its core: what *is* the deeper "yes" burning

My wife's family were refugees. They came to this country as "displaced persons" after World War II. They approached their economic realities with an oft-repeated family mantra, "We're rich; we just don't have a lot of money." They never forgot how to throw really good parties, either! I love my wife's family.

inside of you? By whatever name—passion, lifework, a sense of purpose and meaning—your "yes" is the primary guide for making life's most basic decisions, the ones that make possible the other decisions. Among all the less-important priorities in your life, this "yes" is always in play. Let me give you some examples:

- If your deeper "yes" is to empathize with others, then you most likely seek to know and serve others before you want to be known and served by them.
- If you are most mindful of your own inferiorities, then your "yes" can help diminish those self-diminishing feelings.
- If having fun most fully characterizes you, then anything painful, boring, or ordinary likely comes up as less worthy of your attention.
- If you insist on fairness in all your personal dealings and in all the societal institutions of which you are a part, you are less likely to grouse about injustice.
- If you value personal safety as the primary quality of a good life, then you live and work to protect yourself against any real or imagined danger.

"Yes" or "no" and "enough" are at the heart of simplicity because they signal your basic attitudes about life, the mindfulness by which you approach decisions, and the directions in which those decisions will take you.

Distinguishing among "Yes," "No," and "Enough"

"Yes" or "no" and "enough" are at the heart of simplicity. Together they can form the core of your appreciative conversations with others. But how do you discern among them? Let me tell you about some of the aphorisms that help me sort these three basic decision-making processes in my life.

1. Sometimes "enough" sounds like "Alleluia!" As evidence of gospel grace, "enough" reminds me of the blessing of sufficiency: "Yes, dear God, you have given me just what I need to live life to your glory." "Enough" also reminds me that God does not choose to overburden me unnecessarily or beyond my capacity.

2. "Enough" and "no" can sing together. In my life, no second helpings at supper, no fatty snacks, no carbonated beverages, and no excuses for not exercising have helped me stay fit and healthy. Temptations to excess, busyness, or an overwrought sense of my importance or lifework—all are diminished when my self-talk goes something like, "No, thank you. I already have enough."

3. "Enough," "yes," and "no" can show your integrity. Lived out consistently, each of the three words helps you match your values with your behaviors. Understanding each of these words requires your intellectual and emotional honesty. Pretense about not knowing the meaning of these three concepts is as transparent as trying to patronize a teenager.

4. Eventually "enough" wins. When all is said and done, you are not God, and so you can't do everything all at once, every time, and everywhere. Messing with "enough" brings consequences: You work too hard for too long and you get sick. You don't brush your teeth enough

～✺～

A great civilization is not conquered from without until it has
destroyed itself from within.
—Will Durant

～✺～

and you get gum disease. You accumulate too much stuff
and most of it requires too much time for maintenance,
repair, or disposal.

5. "Enough" sometimes precedes "yes." Alcoholics know
that when you finally hit bottom—ENOUGH in big letters—you are ready to start on the road to sobriety. When a
nation finally has had enough of its leaders or their values,
the people first say "no" to their supposed leaders but then
reach with their votes towards a more joyful "yes." The
sighs of "enough" can lay the foundation for the grateful
tears of "Yes!"

How do you discern which of these three words is operating?
The secret: when one is operating in your life, most likely the other
two are working, too. They form a triumvirate of mutual support,
each for the other. For example, if I don't know whether to say yes
or no to another invitation to speak, I ask myself if I have enough
to do or if I am satisfied with the amount of attention I am already
getting.

For years I carried two smooth touchstones at all times. One I
named "Enough" and the other "Forgive." It was amazing to me
how many times those two concepts, alone or in tandem, helped
me take stock of my feelings, an experience, or a severe challenge.
In the simple act of touching the Enough stone, I often reminded
myself of God's promise, "My grace is sufficient for you" (2 Cor.
12:9 NRSV), and Forgive helped me get over the times when I
didn't live as though "enough" was enough.

～✦～

My wife's father was a factory owner in Warsaw during World War II. He helped Jews escape Hitler's clutches, escaped to Austria before the Warsaw Uprising, and later came to the United States with not much more than his family and a few suitcases. I've often wondered how he remained faithful to his God after so much adversity. I'm pretty sure that when he died he was satisfied with his life.

～✦～

The Power of Gospel Living

It would be easy to think of simplicity as a lifestyle switch permanently fixed in the NO position. That way of living can be seen in the tenets of fundamentalism, which draws its adherents into frames of mind that fear, abhor, or avoid many elements of life. But lifestyles based only on "Thou shalt not" break down soon enough and lose their sensitivity to God's abundance. When any part of a law-only system—law enforcer, judge, jury, jailer—loses its power, law-based lifestyles can't fulfill their promise of a meaningful, purposeful life.

A better way of thinking about simple living is to name it "Good News." Another way to think of gospel-powered living: the salvation after God's salvation. Still another: playing with the Spirit's gifts. Or perhaps: your brain hooked on God's will. Freedom, joy, mission, creativity, courage—all gospel words—give voice to your feelings when you understand that simple living is the result of God's saving you from trying to save yourself. God's fierce repudiation of a fear-based life helps you defy death's hold on your emotions. When fear of dying—or any of its ugly stepchildren—doesn't control your lifestyle, you are freed from its power.

～◇～

Stop for a Moment

Use your computer's search engine to find some blogs (from "Web logs," a kind of online journal) written by folks who think enough of themselves and others to share their thoughts about lifestyle. Do the same with MySpace or Google videos. Try key words like "simplicity," "simple living," or "lifestyle." Some of the bloggers, MySpacers, and videographers think beyond themselves while others are bound up in their own wants and needs. Read a few days' worth of these writings and note the number and tone of the responses to these bloggers. For another stab at this activity, insert the word *Jesus* into the set of key words for your search and see what else happens. What do you notice as you compare these blogs and the reactions they elicit?

～◇～

Managing a Sustainable Life

Let's move now from thinking about the theological dimensions of simplicity to consideration of simplicity as a spiritual practice. We will start with the idea that simple living helps you manage your life over a long period of time. Let me start with a personal story from my dusty past.

In my days as a director of Christian education and youth in a congregation in Austin, Texas, I figured out that most congregational systems were difficult to manage. Sunday schools; congregational boards and committees; funding mechanisms; stable,

⌒≍⌒

*Survey the normal programs or activities of your congregation,
rating them on a scale that gauges each one's capability to equip
congregation members to live more manageable lives. Talk with
other leaders about what you find.*

⌒≍⌒

growing, or maturing membership—each of these systems required
large amounts of social and financial capital to keep running. Like
herding cats, dissembling congregations and their complicated
systems seems to occur more easily than assembling them.

In my leadership in that congregation, I always felt like Sisy-
phus pushing virtual rocks up mythological hills, doomed to fail if
I ever stopped resisting the gravity of the situation. With scores of
other leaders, I worked long hours and most weekends to manage
the interlocking systems of education and youth ministry. As long
as we worked hard enough, we managed the situation well enough
to keep it going long enough. Manageability was a prerequisite
for sustainability. If we couldn't manage a thing, it didn't last very
long.

What I learned over time, though, was that I could not sustain
the high energy and constant attention required to manage these
systems. I am certain that I pushed several congregation leaders to
the brink of burnout; others kept at our grand schemes but were
perpetually tired. Still others came to resent the go-go-go of those
high-energy systems and the toll their volunteer work took on their
family or personal lives. Clearly, I couldn't have kept those systems
running without a constant infusion of new volunteers willing to
pick up what others had let go.

Eventually I ran out of those volunteers, came close to burnout
myself, and came to see that the congregational systems were not
manageable in their complexity and so could not be sustained for
very long. I left that congregation vaguely aware I had to conceive

Several of the simple-living people I know are writers, others poets. Perhaps words are both sanctuaries and protectors for those who are mindful about their ways of living. As a writer I'd like to think that's true.

a simpler way to "do church" and a simpler way to manage the rest of my life.

All these years later, I think I understand the connection between manageable and sustainable, whether in congregations or in your personal life: you can sustain what you can manage. Part of the joy—and perhaps the lure—of simple living is that you choose to manage only what lies within the scope of your actual capabilities and not to live under the pretext of unlimited assets or "purpose-greed"—wanting to fulfill all God's commands for the entire Christian church. The result of that choice: a life that's possible, and a life that lasts.

The Examined Life Is Worth Living

This ever happen to you? You are rushing around too fast, keeping too many balls in the air, too many plates spinning, and trying to explain these impossibilities as multitasking. In that state of mind (or mindlessness?) you make a minor error, which quickly grows into a monstrous mistake that threatens to eat you for lunch. You blame yourself for the growing difficulty or see yourself as flotsam and jetsam on the tides of life. In the middle of the escalating problem—now named as "The Time That Bob Screwed Up an Entire Event by Forgetting to Bring the Handouts"—you don't recall that the whole thing started because you didn't take enough time to think about what you were doing.

～✕～

Speed bump—anything in life that alerts you when you're mov-
ing too fast with too much stuff in your trunk and not enough
brains in your head.

～✕～

Mindless thought—not really an oxymoron when you think about it—characterizes more and more of our lives every day. I am struck, for example, by how much of the work that's done in my ministry is characterized by first drafts and quick glances masquerading as quality and depth. More often than I would like, precious wisdom is available only in small pieces, carried precariously by short bursts of attention.

Simple living counteracts this characteristic of modern life. When you live simply, you choose a way of being and acting in which you discipline yourself—and your self-talk—toward mindfulness, or thinking about your thinking. It takes time for your brain to focus attention around its own perceptions and decisions, so you choose to examine your life just a little more slowly, a little more calmly. You spend more time finding and using your mental maps—your brain's way of collecting its work in efficient clumps of activity—so that the words you say and the decisions you make come from more parts of your brain than the Plate-Spinning Center. You remember the handouts for the event you are supposed to lead.

～✕～

Stop for a Moment

On a piece of paper, list all the major and minor ways you might describe God's call for your life. Name each as an action—for example, "Fighting injustice alongside Latinos" or "Inviting more Latinos into this congregation." Now go through your list and rate realistically how well-equipped you are—by virtue of your available assets—to fulfill each of those life purposes. (Use a scale of 0 to 10, with 0 meaning "not equipped at all" and 10 meaning "very well equipped.") When you are finished with the rating, show it to someone who knows you well and talk together about what patterns you see. For example, group all the life purposes with a rating of 9 or 10, as well as those with a 0 or 1. Talk about well you manage each of these purposes, which purposes may never be fulfilled, or which you might want to let go of. How does your capacity to manage a life purpose mesh with the likelihood that it will continue?

~~~

What Holds Your Attention?

One way you can measure your practice of simplicity is by answering this question: what holds your attention? Jesus put the matter nicely: "Your heart will always be where your treasure is" (Matt. 6:21). Here's a little lesson in New Testament Greek: *thesauros* (treasure) denotes both valued things and the box or receptacle in which they are placed. The location of your treasure influences where your *kardia* (heart) is located. *Heart* was the first century way of describing the center of your will, understanding, motivation, purposes, intelligence, or affections. One way to translate Jesus's words might be: "The box in which you place your treasure is also the place where you put your brain."

Your attention is literally *held* by your treasure. (And for heaven's sake, don't misquote that passage so that "your treasure

~~≈~~

Make a list of adjectives that indicate positive reactions or pleasure. (For example, delightful, pleasing, hopeful.) With list in hand, find some small element in your present lifestyle—a can of food or phone conversations—and see which of the adjectives you can legitimately use to describe that item or element of life. What would happen if you did this for everything you encounter?

~~≈~~

is where your heart is." That's not what Jesus said.) Jesus understood that your mind has a way of being influenced heavily by your surroundings. Given the way your brain works, pleasurable stuff easily holds your attention. Your emotions and values also come along with your attention, as do your behaviors and even your identity.

For the most part, though, you can still choose where to put your treasure. Most folks call that choice "paying attention." The way your brain works is that you give that attention to only one thing at a time. After a while, what you pay attention to gradually determines what you will *not* pay attention to. (Jesus again: "You cannot be the slave of two masters!" [Matt. 6:24].)

So as you consider the way you live, you can judge it as joyfully simple, satisfying, and manageable by the amount and quality of the attention you devote to various aspects of your life. (You can also measure the simplicity of your life by what you choose *not* to attend to.)

Here's an example from my daily life: Chris and I have come to see that dinnertime is a precious opportunity to converse together earnestly and quietly about what's important in our lives and our relationship. Because we want to hold each other's attention while we eat and talk, we do not watch television news, read magazines, answer the phone, or listen to National Public Radio.

~⚜~

*The trouble with simple living is that, though it can be joyful,
rich, and creative, it isn't simple.*
—*Attributed to Doris Janzen Longacre*

~⚜~

Our conversations are graced by humor, depth, and honesty. We measure our dinnertimes not by an increased knowledge of world news but by the bonds of friendship, decision making, or shared wisdom that hold our attention during supper. We could describe our treasures and our hearts as the gifts of delicious food, delightful conversation, precious insight, and quiet laughter that are held on a dinner plate, the end of a fork, and the sparkle in each other's eyes. Our relationship, not our television, holds our attention.

Simplicity as a Direction

An axiom of spiritual practices is that they enable the direction of a journey instead of naming its destination. Holding that distinction in mind can keep you from unnecessarily harsh judgments about yourself. A colleague who lives very simply once astounded me by announcing that she still wasn't satisfied with the simplicity of her life because her schedule was not manageable. I was surprised because this person seemed to be a paragon of all the virtues of simple living. Her response to my surprise: she assured me that at least she was heading in the right direction.

I have kept that idea in mind as I have tried to evaluate the way I live my life. In living simply I find it more realistic to name the direction—less is more—than to name its destination by some standard of perfection. Perhaps this is a subtle way by which I make excuses for my lifestyle, but it's also a way to keep me from overwhelming self-incrimination.

In the first decades of the simple-living movement, self-righteousness was sometimes easy to find. I remember during one period of drought in northern California how proud I was that our family was using gray water—carried in buckets—to water our garden. I also recall my quiet disdain of people who discharged their washing-machine rinse water into the sewers of the Bay Area. I thought that the end results of my kind of simplicity were better than others' simplicity. Nowadays? I am satisfied if I can find a few folks heading in the same direction, thinking of water as a precious resource to be shepherded carefully.

As You Move Forward

Now that you have considered some theological and practical fundamentals about living simply, you are getting closer to starting simplicity conversations in your congregation. When you eventually engage the people in your congregation, I hope you can characterize simplicity as more than a harsh attack on every aspect of life in the Western world. Instead, try to convey to others that this way of thinking and behaving is helpful, life sustaining, deeply spiritual, and eminently possible. In that way, you will help others see simplicity as it really is. You will help them find simplicity itself.

～✦～

Stop for a Moment

Psycholinguists have for years theorized that our words determine our thoughts, not the other way around. The way we use words certainly reveals what we think but also shapes the thoughts themselves. This means that analyzing—and possibly changing—the words you use to describe your lifestyle can be helpful for you. Think about these ideas:

- If you use mostly passive words and constructs, you are likely thinking you are a victim of circumstance, someone who floats wherever the currents of life take you. To live simply you want to be active, to swim—perhaps against the tide—instead of going with the flow.

- Think about words you use that contradict simplicity. An example: do you "run errands" or "run to the store" when you could as easily say, "do errands" or "go to the store"?

- How often do you use "more" or "better" as a reason to buy or do something? For example: your toothbrush works fine, but you are persuaded to purchase an electric one because your dentist says that it works better. Or think about the possibly frenetic activities of your congregation's evangelism or stewardship committees as they seek more members and more money. What is a more joyful way to live that doesn't always rely on "more," "better," and their ilk?

3

Hold On

~~~

I am an asset-based-thinking kind of guy, so I don't like to wait around for a needs-based thinking, nit-picking analysis of "the problems we face" or the proper application of SWOT (Strengths, Weaknesses, Opportunities, Threats) analysis to strategic planning. Instead, I like to gather the gifts God offers me, tinker with them a bit, assemble them into useful constructions, and get to work alongside other gifted and giving people.

On the One Hand, Homegrown Barriers

After thinking about simple living for all these years, though, I am coming to see that the smallest things can keep people from moving their lives from the fast lane to a more sustainable pace, carrying fewer possessions along the way. Sometimes their beliefs are what trip them up. So in this chapter I want to help you recognize what may stand in your way so that you will know what these self-made barriers might look like. When I am finished naming these stumbling blocks, I will tell you some ways you can work around them.

This approach doesn't mean that I am going to abandon my usual asset-based thinking and focus on The Problems. One thing I have learned about problems or barriers: they are also assets—useful gifts—because they can serve as motivators for your

God can bless you with everything you need, and you will always have more than enough to do all kinds of good things for others.

—*2 Corinthians 9:8*

actions. Just like problems may compel you to find solutions, so barriers might provoke some barrier-busting gene in your brain. Maybe you and I are alike in this regard: tell me that something can't be done, that the rules don't allow such-and-such, that *appropriate* is an über-adjective, or that I must continue to wait for the right moment—and I will probably begin considering how to go over, under, around, or through those barriers. That's how I would like you to think about the following listing of the personally constructed barriers that might deter you from living simply. So that you can remember them more easily, I have framed each barrier by a short statement about the personal values that may lie at the heart of the barriers.

Stop for a Moment

Before you get started on this chapter, take a piece of scratch paper and scribble some quick notes about this question: what stands in the way of your living more simply, more fully, more joyfully? If the piece of blank paper deters your creativity or honesty, ask someone who loves you to help you scratch on the scratch paper.

~~~~

According to the National Association of Home Builders, homes built in 2006 are, on average, 40 percent bigger than homes built 30 years ago.

~~~~

You May Want to Be God

Martin Luther was right: in many ways, the First Commandment is the only commandment. If you think *you* are God, then deep in your heart you also think that everything belongs to you. You build your own temple or starter castle—and, for heaven's sake, you find just the right breed of dog to match that house. You get what you want, you set up your own rules. You are the subject of all your sentences, you choose whom to ignore or condemn; you gather the praise and affirmations you so rightly deserve; you answer to yourself first of all. You are a brand of One, after all, and you have the right to choose those on whom you will dispense your favors.

The Big Guy and Jesus? Friends of yours. The church? A good place to do business and slurp up those accolades. Your family? Evidence of your godly authority. All your stuff? The necessary supplies you need to remind yourself and others of your power and authority.

This is a very convenient way of thinking and very easy to understand; it's problematic only when you discover all around you the clueless people who for some odd reason think that *they* are God.

You May Be Addicted

It doesn't take much—toys, love, heroin, alcohol, sexual activity, entertainment, food, apparel catalogs—for your brain to squirt its nucleus accumbens full of pleasure-inducing neurotransmitters—chemical messengers that help the brain do its work. This pleasure center of the human brain then asks for a simple favor: "Can I have some more of the same, please?" Once satisfied by the pleasure-causing substance or action, your brain is thereafter satisfied only with "again" and "more." That's the way addiction works, fed by your overfascination with things, speeded-up lifestyles, risky relationships, and any substances or experiences that bring a rush of sheer pleasure. Once these patterns become habits, the brain structures that ask for pleasure also take charge of the rest of your brain, pushing aside many other motivations and ways of thinking. "More" becomes the monkey on your back.

Fear of Death Compels You

Thirty years ago I was writing a curriculum for children about caring for the environment. In my background research I found general agreement that one of the major causes for the deterioration of the world's climate and resources was relentless consumption of goods. I also read that the ultimate motivation for this materialism or consumerism is fear of death. It seemed an astounding, even preposterous, notion at the time, but not so anymore. Over the past thirty years, I have also been reading about brain science, and fear keeps popping up almost everywhere as a primary explanation for many of life's most basic—and sometimes stupidest—decisions. Even though people know that some of their actions are really dumb and ultimately useless, they still foul their own nests with stuff and ruin their health with hyperactive lifestyles. Death? If people move fast enough and surround themselves with enough stuff, they won't have time or reason to think about it.

Fear of death is instantaneous, persistent, overwhelming, and subtle. Fear of growing older, fear of illness, fear of being

~~~❦~~~

The greatest way to show love for friends is to die for them.

—*John 15:13*

~~~❦~~~

ignored, and fear of poverty—this family of feelings can motivate you, quickly and dependably. Manufacturers and their marketers know how easily you can be persuaded to buy their products because you fear bad breath, wrinkles, diminished sexual appetite, crooked teeth, or thinning hair. Manipulative politicians and preachers can scare you into action more quickly and more assuredly than if they try to inspire you to do something. When you are captured by fear, you may try to avoid its clutches by living inside the protective shell of your home or car or cubicle. You may think like a hermit crab, reaching out gingerly with a claw to grab only what happens to land within the circle of your grasp.

Like the name of a scandalous relative, *death* is a word you probably don't bring up in polite company. Instead, you may talk about price-busting bargains and sales, the excellent quality of your possessions, the exquisite pleasure of shopping for its own sake. You might fill your Christmas newsletter with accounts of your adventures and accomplishments while leaving out your failures and sorrows. You may avoid people who are poor—you don't need reminding how vulnerable your family finances are—and you may keep your closets full of new clothes so that you will feel new and young instead of used and old.

Sadly—even among Christians who follow a Savior who conquered death and who promises life that doesn't end—even in our own company of godly people this fear is a silent presence.

~≫≪~

Stop for a Moment

Make tomorrow a Fear-Filter day: keep a running tally of the times you encounter something or someone that adds fear to your life. And think about this question: how might this simple tallying help you filter out fear?

~≫≪~

You'd Still Like to Be Popular

I was not one of the popular kids in high school. At 95 pounds dripping wet, I was not exactly football or soccer material. I played the pipe organ instead of the guitar, I started going bald at age 16, and I never learned to dance. I remember the feeling of being on the outside of the circles of popularity looking in. I recall how difficult it was for me to decide whether I wanted to break into those circles.

Perhaps you also remember a time in your life when you wanted desperately to be known as one of the popular kids; you may recall some of the things you were willing to do to be known and appreciated by them. The mental tapes of those times in your life may still play in your brain. (Note to self: change "tapes" metaphor to "files on a two-gigabyte flash drive.")

If you were one of the small group of perpetual insiders, partygoers, fashion goddesses, or invisible leaders, you may still know how to maintain your status through your lifestyle. And if you weren't one of the way-cool kids, you may still be trying to make up for lost ground. Moving fast and piling up stuff may now seem like good ways to finally achieve your popularity goals from yesteryear. Only now, being popular may cost you more money,

∼≷∽

Our daughter came home from her first days of kindergarten complaining that other kids were examining the labels of her clothing to see where her parents shopped. We knew it was a snobby, classist thing; we also knew that we bought most of her clothing from a really nice thrift store with really high-class clothing (and labels). We solved the dilemma by cutting off all the tags. To this day, our daughter remains difficult to label.

∼≷∽

time, and attention in order to get what you have wanted all these years. Now the popular kids may be the Joneses, all of them.

So you know, I chose *not* to be popular or to seek the favor of those folks and found instead a collection of other nonpopulars with whom to spend my time. It turned out to be a good choice, because out of that experience I learned to be satisfied with whatever attention I get from anyone. Both the popular and the not-so-popular people. Sadly, though, I still don't know how to dance.

You Want to Follow the Leader(s)

Daniel Goleman's *Social Intelligence: The New Science of Human Relationships* (New York: Bantam Books, 2006) adds compelling detail to his earlier writing about "emotional intelligence." Now, says Goleman, the way the human brain behaves in relationships can be seen more clearly, and it appears that this form of intelligence may be hardwired in the brain. Other researchers have described this form of intelligence as the work of mirror neurons deep down inside of your brain. These brain cells have probably been present ever since you were born and help you to mimic actions—and perhaps feelings—that you see. For babies

~~❦~~

Don't be stupid and believe everything you hear; be smart and
know where you are headed.
—Proverbs 14:15

~~❦~~

and children this is a good skill—you start learning to survive by seeing and doing, long before you learn the words that describe these actions.

Because you are a social animal, you can also read faces with some skill. In a fraction of a second, you choose from among scores of possible meanings you see in the faces of another person and with amazing precision can usually choose correctly the emotion or state of mind that the faces of others communicate.

Your capacity for mimicry might create one small problem for simple living, though: it's possible that you also use these skills in a naive and compliant response to suggestion, especially from respected—or feared—people who you consider leaders. I see this all around me almost every day. Otherwise thoughtful people agree to undertake projects, viewpoints, alliances, or emotions that they later admit are harmful, overburdening, wrong, or stupid. Why? Simply because they were mimicking the behavior of someone with supposed authority. In my world, meetings seem to be the place where this power of suggestion—or verbal mimicry—seems to operate best.

Although you might see mimicry like immature peer pressure that goes away when your adolescent skin problems clear up, the truth might lie in the opposite direction: you might become very, very good at reading the faces of those whose approval you seek and you might grow highly skilled in responding favorably to their suggestions in order to obtain their favor. You might also become especially skilled in copying—why *do* we call it "aping"?—the behavior of others you perceive as leaders, even when you know it to be wrong or self-destructive.

~≈~

Construct a conceptual map of all the subjects that connect with simple living. For starters, think of the environment, satisfaction, children's allowances, greed, happiness, fear of death, and Jesus's lifestyle. Post your map somewhere where you can add to it as you read this book.

~≈~

You Don't Hear or Read about Simplicity

Psycholinguists have for years suggested that the richness and skill by which you use words is connected to the richness and skill of your thought processes. An easier way to remember this idea: know words, know thoughts; no words, no thoughts.

The barrier to simple living? In your daily life, not many places exist where you come upon words—spoken, written, pixellated—about living simply. In fact, the opposite is true. Because not even Oprah can make money on promoting truly simple living, these themes aren't going to be driven by society's word-spewing machinery. Because people who live simply usually do so quietly—or at least unnoticed—you are not going to read their life stories on the pages of entertainer-enriched supermarket checkout tabloids. Because simplicity by its nature requires fewer words than complexity, the whole subject just doesn't get its share of attention in the word-seeking parts of your brain.

One of the reasons I am filling this book with many different kinds of words for your eyes and brain is because I want you to have a rich vocabulary from which you can think about simplicity. This is also why I am hoping you will take the words of this book into heartfelt conversations with people you know and love.

The Right Time Never Comes for You

My wife and I have lived frugally since we were first married. That's why we could afford to live below the federal poverty line for a

Magazine publishers are asking me to renew my subscriptions more frequently, out into the next decade. Are publishers running out of "now," or do they think I've lost track of the time?

while, why we could be generous when it came to our children's well-being, and why we could enjoy a fairly manageable lifestyle all these years. One problem, though: we didn't really start to carefully budget our income or saving for our retirement until much later in our marriage. We were waiting for the right time.

Like budgeting or saving, living simply can easily be left on its simple-but-elegant pedestal in the Hall of Good Intentions in your life. Like "being more generous" or "spending more time with good friends," this ideal way to live stands quietly on its marble perch, waiting for just the right circumstances. But because the right moments never quite gel completely, you can easily avoid the insistent discipline that seems to underlie simple living. Waiting—sometimes thought of as wisdom—in this case becomes an invisible barrier you make for yourself.

You might wait for optimum spirituality, more settled schedules for your kids, a carefully cultivated set of friends, well-considered hobbies, just the right stage in life and, of course, the little cabin in the forested glen. But while you work on shaping one factor, the others slip away like too many cookies in a child's hand. And while waiting for the factors to accumulate into a cohesive whole, you might get used to lifestyles that are anything but simple.

I know about this because Chris and I *did* live in that little cabin, we *did* cultivate just a few important hobbies—have I told you about my firewood gathering?—and we *did* become part of a Christian commune, presumably to find spiritual maturity. But even that quiet life was not completely simple, because the commune turned into a messy set of relationships, the little cabin kept needing major repairs, and we burned up all the firewood every year. And we still had not learned to discipline ourselves to a budget or save money for our later years. The lesson we learned there was that avoidance of complicated lifestyles is not the same as seeking simplicity.

~~~

Stop for a Moment

Think about this question: when it comes to living more simply, what are you waiting for? Give each of your reasons a fanciful name, just so you remember that delaying simplicity until "just the right time in life" may be a bit silly.

~~~

You Like to Keep Things to Yourself

Here's a strange circumstance in contemporary culture: at the same time that we demand absolute transparency of our leaders, our movie stars, and our pastors, we insist that our own privacy is an inalienable right. I experience this desire for privacy from my life inside the wonderful bureaucracy where I work. The maxim "There are no secrets here" is something I believe about other people's lives. But I somehow maintain the illusion that my life—including my secret hopes and sins—is unknown to the people around me. Another illusion I live with: that in the public arenas of the church I can influence others while striving to keep my private life, my witness, my foibles, and my passions hid from my colleagues and the people I serve.

When it comes to how you spend down your income and use up your time, that insistence on privacy may keep you from being

~~≈~~

Contrary to popular belief, you are not what you drive.
—From a Citigroup "Live Richly" billboard

~~≈~~

accountable to others who could help you. The secrecy with which you guard your life also deprives you of the counsel of heads wiser than your own, and keeps you locked inside the traps and temptations of profligacy and acquisitiveness.

You Hope to Be a Winner

Decision and glory theology pervades the church these days. It's a brand of theology that infers that your good and godly actions eventually lead toward victories, success, or other rewards for you. (And you want to be a winner, don't you?) Whether it's Calvinism run amuck (an interesting word picture) or Lutheranism set free (another possible oxymoron?), this brand of thinking runs into simple living like a runaway truck plowing into a flock of free-range chickens who were busy discussing Wendell Berry's poetry while waiting to cross the road.

Here's how this kind of theology works against your valuing simple living: simple living doesn't seem like a touchdown, a Big Win, or a triumph against much of anything. Laced with sports metaphors like a turkey pumped full of basting broth, triumphal notions of the Christian life don't readily match the principles and results of simple living. For example, congregations filled with Winners might have difficulty foregoing the big auditorium on the big campus in favor of renting space and giving away most of their offerings to the poor. At a personal level, Winners might have difficulty accepting as their reward for good living a quiet little bungalow in a middle-ring suburb, with a ten-year-old Chevy in the carport instead of a starter castle in an outer-ring suburb, with a riding lawnmower larger than most homes in China.

~~~

Sometimes my father would use strange tools to do simple jobs. Once my brothers and I found him using a pipe wrench to pound nails. When we asked him why he wasn't using a hammer, he responded, "Too easy." I've always thought a lesson was in there somewhere.

~~~

In this strange strain of Christian theology, victories are by their nature large and attention-getting phenomena. In this way of thinking, *small* means "loser" and *humble* means "not accepting the gracious abundance that God so bountifully outpours on His righteous disciples." Winners and losers deserve what they get. Sorry, but in my experience, simple living and this brand of Christianity probably don't easily validate each other. I could be wrong, and very well may be a Loser, because I have fired myself from two jobs—I closed a school and a federally funded job-training program—and still don't have an iPod or a plasma-screen home auditorium.

You Value Your Tools, Even When They Harm You

Many social critics have noted that once you accept the validity of any technology, it begins to place demands on your activities. This phenomenon is part of the Law of Unintended Consequences. If you have a hammer, you not only hammer in the morning, but everything looks like a nail. If you have a car—especially if you are 16 and have "earned" the car by working 20 hours a week in the burgeoning pizza-delivery business—you may have to keep working at that job to pay for insurance, repairs, fuel, and other doodads that make your car a Really Cool Artifact of your all-around worth and attractiveness. You might automatically drive to places you could walk to, shop anywhere and everywhere the car can go, or put your kids in traveling sports leagues that suck up your Sunday mornings.

~•~

Security is mostly a superstition. It does not exist in nature. . . .
Life is either a daring adventure or nothing at all.

—*Helen Keller*

~•~

Another ordinary example: clothes require closets and hangers, dry-cleaning, and dryer sheets that eliminate static cling and add the smell of questionable chemicals to your body. The more clothes you buy, the more space they take up; the more washing, ironing, and folding time they require; the more you attend to the fashion consciousness that required their purchase in the first place.

In your congregation, large projection screens eventually require larger projectors, brighter bulbs, more connecting wires, more complex software, extra technical training, not to mention the possible redesign of your entire worship space to accommodate the new technology and its necessary security paraphernalia. A pipe organ requires tuning, a special type of musician, and the same kind of security system. A computerized member database requires constant debugging and updating.

At worst, your tools may be a harsh mistress or master. At best, they pry time and attention away from other, perhaps-more-important facets of your daily living. Many of your tools promise more efficient lifestyles, but end up saving, for the worst possible moments, the dreaded command, "You will please repair me. Now!"

You Believe in Precise Planning

Simple living just doesn't make the grade with those who demand certain, measurable precision in their work, relationships, and hopes. If you are one of those folks—you actually believe that you can plan your work and work your plan—you can be put off by a

---

Look into a mirror as though you were an outside-the-mirror observer of yourself. What joys and sorrows do you see? What could you learn from this mirror person? What do these eyes tell you? How would you describe this person, just by looking at this face? What questions would you like to ask the person in the mirror?

---

way of thinking about life that's not predictable or easily quantified. Truth be told, when it comes to simplicity no definitive measures for your success or failure exist, no progression from benchmark to benchmark, no International Standards Organization (ISO) standards.

Instead of approaching life like it's a problem that can be solved with good planning, simple-living adherents work from intuition and relationships—notably imprecise qualities of life. Sometimes they trust conversation over planning, risk-filled ventures instead of surefire techniques, and emergent possibilities rather than cause-and-effect thinking.

Stop for a Moment

How are you doing with these beliefs that work against simple living? Anything familiar in any of this? Any misgivings about my warnings? Take up your trusty pen or pencil and scribble into the margins some of your thoughts about what you have read so far so that you have ample material for the conversations that you and I hope will take place in your congregation.

*Approach any object you encounter today with these questions:
How did this remarkable thing get here? By whose hand and
mind was this formed? What will become of it next?*

You May Think Only Strange People Live Simply

Simple living has long been treated with subtle, quiet disregard
and outright resistance. This can work against its widespread
approval in the general population. Well-intentioned folks have
disagreed with some of the economic tenets of simple living—what
will happen to the job market if folks buy hardly anything?—and
some have thought of simplicity proponents as mere hermits or
tree huggers.

This history works against the adoption of simple lifestyles
because these prejudices may have become an accepted way of
thinking among people whose economic self-interest seems threat-
ened by the propositions of simple living. I remember distinctly
the moment several years ago when I proposed to my colleagues
adding "simple living" to my personal work plan and job description. They were hesitant about the matter because, in the early days
of the simplicity movement, it was connected to hippies, Eastern
religions, and the Jesus Movement. As you might guess, simple
living did *not* get added to my work plan or job description. As
you might not guess, I switched jobs.

You May Feel Guilty about Not Living Simply

This statement reveals one of the major reasons why most people
don't want to try living simply. When I talk to most folks, this is
what I hear almost immediately: a guilt-infested litany about the

～≳≺～

*Hedonophobia—the fear of feeling pleasure. Sometimes incor-
rectly associated with simple living.*

～≳≺～

ways in which they use too much electricity, waste water, and move
through life at a frenetic clip. This confession is quickly followed
by expressions of culpability and vague notions of how they probably *should* change something or other in their lives. This is hardly
a joyful approach to life.

If I would stay at the level of "Shame on you, Bob Sitze, for
owning a car that does not run on cow manure," I would be accepting guilt as a legitimate—albeit momentary—motivator for
mindless reactions such as "Gee, maybe I *should* collect cattle from
the surrounding countryside and pile their droppings into a four-
thousand-dollar Acme Methane Converter for my mini-SUV."

Shame and guilt don't work very well as motivation for simple
living. Neither works well over the long haul, and both create their
own resistance: avoiding the source of the discomfort. Using shame
and guilt is no way to build a lasting movement of God's people
committed to the joyful possibilities God has in mind for just and
sustainable lifestyles.

You Don't Expect Simplicity to Be Joyful

One of the prejudices about simplicity is that it consists mainly
of giving up everything. If you buy into this view of simplicity,
grim-facedness can become your preferred visage and Jeremiah
your favorite prophet. If, at the opposite end of the emotional
spectrum, you live in a world where pleasure is Queen or Princess,
you don't want to be the churlish knave at the bottom of the
castle, mucking around in the mud with pigs, when you could be

The next time you're waiting—in an airport, standing in line at the market, waiting for a street signal to change—take a quick look around you for evidence of people enjoying life in simple ways.

at the top of the castle eating roast pork, dancing the night away, or generally carrying on. If fun is the good-life thing you seek, then doing without—whether real or imagined—takes away the fun. Unless, of course, you are really into mud.

If you believe that simplicity is based on scarcity or some form of ascetic righteousness—and therefore joyless—you will likely not want to engage in it, except if you are forced to do so by circumstance. Again, this attitude misses the truth that God wants us to live abundantly.

Stop for a Moment

You have finished *my* list of the barriers to living simply that any of us might construct, but my guess is that you know more of them. Before you move to the next section—where we will talk about how to move past barriers—think about what I have left out, glossed over, treated too lightly, or missed by a mile. Use the margins here to name more of your barriers to living simply. Try my one-sentence-adage naming method.

On the Other Hand, Homegrown Breezeways

You have been patient while I have trotted out my rogues' gallery of the barriers that might keep you from connecting your identity, feelings, or behaviors with simple living. Let's turn now (finally, Bob!) to some of the ways by which you can move over, under, around, or through these and other barriers. I hope you are ready for some practical, hopeful ways to think and act, some of them already known to you and some as close as the nearest horizon in your life. Once again, I will present them as short statements so that you can remember these ideas.

You Can "Win" Over the Long Haul

Every player, coach, and water carrier on every team anywhere in the world has probably won at least one game, bout, match, set, or contest. That's not really victory, though, because one game does not make a season or a sports dynasty. What's true about simple living is that it allows for long-term success. Here's how that works:

Let's say that in your latter years you decide to buy a red sports car and adopt gold chains and a spiffy pseudo-outdoorsperson wardrobe as your preferred fashion. You win in this lifestyle decision as long as the car runs, the gold chain doesn't get stolen at the gym where you work out to remain buff, and the wardrobe doesn't get moose stew all over it. (I am told that red-sports-car-owning, pseudo-outdoors people eat a lot of moose stew.) For the few moments when you get the admiring-but-fleeting looks of cute women or the oohs and aahs of guys in large gas-sucking SUVs, you are a winner. But down deep—when you are buried in dirty clothes, looking at a $753 bill for replacing the Wiggins Valve on your car, and pawing through your underwear drawer to find the gold chain—you know that the great joy you have felt as

It's much better to be wise and sensible than to be rich.
—*Proverbs 16:16*

New Car and Trendy Clothes Person is as fragile as a soap bubble. At that moment, weighed down by money woes and a detergent that does *not* take out moose stew stains, you know darn well that your short-lived winning also carries a big price tag in your life.

When you live simply, on the other hand, you redefine "winning" so that you are satisfied with less over a longer period of time. So you enjoy your 2002 Chevy Geo because it hardly ever needs repairing, you enjoy your tattered jeans for their lasting comfort and the Nicaraguan yarn friendship bracelet someone gave you as a sign of Christianity's continuing gift of faith and hope in that country. Driving is a pleasure because you are enjoying the scenery and not looking for attention. Your clothes have simple functions and your jewelry makes a statement about something other than you.

In simple living, "winning" turns into "sustainable" and "manageable," and that means you have a better chance of being successful than of trying to make your numbers every quarter, impress everyone you meet, or stay on top of every apparel style that crosses your kitchen table in catalogs with "Wild," "Country," and "Creek" in their titles. So you choose to live beyond the moment, cherishing the prospect that your life will have joy through all its stages, not just the not-yet-mature one.

Which person are you in this story? The winner, of course.

You Have Your Integrity

In *A Generous Presence: Spiritual Leadership and the Art of Coaching* (Alban Institute, 2006), pastor, author, and personal coach

~~❦~~

*Influenczema—an itching disease characterized by the overac-
tive presumptions that you are the influencing factor that causes
other folks to change.*

~~❦~~

Rochelle Melander probes the foundations of caring leadership. She speaks of the value of personal integrity in any relationship. Over and over again, she calls her readers back to the largest and smallest matters that make up integrity. The connection between simplicity and personal integrity is profound: where your life is filled with integrity—your behaviors match your values over a sustained period of time—you can transcend the temptations to forsake who you really are. On the other hand, where your life is filled with nonsustainable complexity—possessions, schedules, expectations—you cannot maintain a cohesive identity, and you are likely torn into little pieces of a You Puzzle that can't ever be put together correctly.

To say this another way, simplicity compels integrity.

You Can Get Good Coaching

Before I let go the subject of integrity, let me talk a little here about life—or lifestyle—coaching, a helpful service of certified professionals whose numbers are growing and whose expertise can be extremely helpful to those wanting to get off fast tracks and to step away from acquisitive notions of the good life. Simple living seems to be the hallmark of their work and in some ways the end result of their efforts.

I know three of these lifestyle coaches personally, and as I hear them talk I get the sense that their work contains something very profound. They aim their considerable wisdom and encouragement at the ordinary places in life where you can get stuck on a small matter that keeps you from maturing or moving any further. A family therapist may concentrate on the deeper questions of human relationships and proven coping strategies. A life coach may start with—and sometimes stay at—prosaic matters of family living that vex you, such as how to declutter physical space, find ways to eat together, think about children's allowances, or negotiate shared household responsibilities.

Like therapists and counselors, life coaches don't live your life for you, and like therapists and counselors, coaches ask probing questions and may offer some advice. What seems to be different among these professions is the point in life where you engage their services. You likely seek a therapist or counselor when you are thinking about getting out of the game or when it's nearly over; you work with a coach so that you can stay in the game. With a counselor or therapist, you learn how to play hurt; with a coach you learn how to avoid injuries.

I am excited about this growing field of helpful professionals. If I were to use a single metaphor to describe the benefits of counselors, therapists, or psychologists as compared to lifestyle coaches, I would equate the first group with doctors and the lifestyle coaches with midwives or nurse-practitioners. In both cases, help is available.

Stop for a Moment

Imagine yourself in conversation with a lifestyle coach. What would you talk about, and what would you keep to yourself for a while? Reverse the roles now and imagine yourself coaching someone who needed help with a lifestyle slowly heading out of control. What questions would you ask, and how might you be helpful?

⌇⌇

*Don't be like the people of this world, but let God change the
way you think.*
—*Romans 12:2*

⌇⌇

You Know Who You Are, and Are Not

If you get trapped in peer approval, one way to counteract that
situation is to remind yourself of how you are different from others.
Without lapsing into holier-than-thou-ness, you take stock of the
ways in which you are *not* like the others, even how you may not
belong in a category of people. The trick, of course, is to maintain
your sense of self while still genuinely loving and accepting others
who are different from you.

Your self-differentiation is helped if you see the Christian life
as essentially positioned as a critique of evil, including self-absorp-
tion, materialism, or any other form of greed or coveting. You
can participate joyfully in all the richness of God's world but still
maintain your responsibility and privilege to reject what destroys
or diminishes that world.

When you think of yourself in these ways, you can avoid
mindlessly absorbing every societal trend or every social pressure.
Despite the possibility that you may invisibly project your dislike
of anyone who does not live simply, you can genuinely approach
any other person with an earnest and loving invitation to live in a
way that really works. You can help people change their lives.

Your Courage Grows Courage

IT TAKES LEATHER BALLS TO PLAY RUGBY. So goes the
semivulgar bumper sticker bragging about this semi-insane sport.
Because of rugby's high rate of serious injuries, I have wondered

❧

Any intelligent fool can make things bigger, more complex, and more violent. It takes a touch of genius—and a lot of courage—to move in the opposite direction.
—E. F. Schumacher

❧

whether that message should actually read, IT TAKES LEATHER BRAINS TO PLAY RUGBY. It also takes a different kind of brain to live simply, one filled with leathery, lasting courage.

Courage begets courage. Once you ratchet up your resolve and face the risks of simplifying one aspect of your life—let's say not coveting what others have—then you are more likely able to find the courage to try some other element of downsizing or rightsizing your lifestyle, perhaps not paying attention to the media that encourage coveting in the first place.

At the start of the book I gave you a picture of myself as a rumpled guy dressed in jeans, hiking shoes, and a tan work shirt and grey hair going in five directions. This is also the way I dress at work. Choosing *not* to wear a bowtie, blue blazer, and dress khakis as my work uniform is a way for me to remember those in the world who have no choice about what they wear, to simplify my wardrobe, and to forsake the bleary-eyed early morning task of finding some article of clothing that will make me look nice. Maybe you see that as cute or at least quaint—eccentrics get to wear purple, or jeans, if they prefer—but in some workplaces I could easily face gentle and quiet disdain because I don't dress "professionally."

Because courage can be its own reward—or at least its own progenitor—one courageous decision to live simply can become the start for a whole series of audacious acts. In my case, a small bit of courage regarding my work attire has strengthened my resolve to approach ordinary working people in ways that show them

❦

You are not silver, gold or platinum. You are you.
—From a Citigroup "Live Richly" billboard

❦

honor and respect and to relate to them directly and honestly. From these relationships, I expect to gather the nerve to approach almost anyone in conversation about their ways of living. Perhaps I will eventually take up rugby.

Your Assets Breed Assets

As I have described, simplicity helps courage grow, but simple living also connects with asset-based planning and asset-based thinking.

In Luther Snow's *The Power of Asset Mapping* (Alban, 2004), you can quickly learn the process of asset mapping. But perhaps more important are Snow's deeper insights about how this planning philosophy can gradually morph into your total approach to life or your way of thinking about almost every situation. Snow understands how people "act their way into thinking." He knows how repeated and thoughtful actions gradually form brain maps—preferred patterns by which the brain processes information—that are the brain's first choice when it encounters a new situation. Once it becomes habitual, an asset-based way of thinking helps you encounter life with increased capabilities and creativity.

How that happens is relatively simple: assets are useful gifts, and when you search for and name them, you find yourself focusing more and more on what is possible and useful instead of what you are missing. Your metaphorical half-empty glasses turn into always-full glasses—half water/half air. You become more adept at problem solving, not by analysis but by quick and effective actions—based on your plentiful assets—that are usually successful.

❧

*Think of your bill-paying time as a ritual of thankfulness for
your financial resources and for the people who offer their services
to you for mere money.*

❧

I remember how asset-based thinking worked into my life after
I first encountered its basic premises. It was about 20 years ago,
and the good folks at the Rodale Institute in Emmaus, Pennsylvania, briefed some of us denominational folks on how they were
helping rural communities around the world with a technique they
called "capacity analysis." (This now-60-year-old institute had for
years focused on food production, environmental concerns, and
health issues and was delving deeper into the broader sociologies
of health and wellness.) The Rodale Institute staff told us stories
of rural communities that learned to discover and use the capacities already existing among their citizens. I was astounded at their
ideas and wondered how they might apply to the workings of
congregations. Another 15 years went by before these concepts
surfaced in my work plan and another couple more years for my
colleagues and me to develop some programs—in stewardship
and hunger education—that took advantage of this effective way
of planning.

Along the way I started noticing some differences in my own
thinking. I began seeing the abundance of blessings in my personal and work situations; gratitude welled up in me more and
more. Increasingly I was able to sense the capacities of others and
to help them discover and use those gifts in tangible ways to accomplish their goals. Under duress or sudden difficulty, I found
myself asking the classic asset-based question, "So, what's useful
here?" and being able to calm myself and others with the assurance
that we could *take advantage* of problems and leverage them into
something useful for God's will.

Because asset-based planning and thinking sidesteps the destructive effects of negativity, complaining, or supposed victimhood, it allows a person's assets to gather other assets like magnets gather iron filings. In workshops around the country, I have watched people discover their useful gifts and put them to work in exciting congregational events, programs, or emphases. Sometimes those assets have lain dormant for years, invisible and therefore not useful. In almost every workshop, I hear the comment, "I didn't know that you could _____" (fill in the blank). Sometimes a single asset causes a sudden bloom of assets in a group as its members discover similar gifts. I have even seen people who have thought of themselves as ordinary or even ungifted perk up with new energy as they survey a map of their assets that fills an entire wall.

Back to simplicity. An asset-based way of planning and thinking counteracts especially well the idea that simplicity is really just throwing away "the good life." Here's how: when you move toward simple living you assess every facet of your life, considering its necessity and its effects. You discover your gifts and also prune away what's unnecessary or problematic. Eventually you come to value what you may have overlooked in the surfeit of possessions and the rush of an overpurposed life.

Asset-based thinking also works against the creeping, creepy idea that more is what you need to get anything done. Asset thinking starts with "I have enough" and so calms your spirit when you start to think of yourself as perpetually needy or living with great-and-continuing deficits. Another capability that asset thinking engenders: the shrewd, bare-knuckles creativity that says, "No matter what I have, I'll make something good out of it."

Jesus Has Been Here Before You

Some of the time I approach the life of Jesus as a gripping story filled with gripping truth. Like the saga of covered-wagon trains in an old Western movie, the Jesus narratives creak their way along

─❧❧─

*You cannot be the slave of two masters. You will like one more
than the other or be more loyal to one than to the other. You
cannot serve God and money.*
—Luke 16:13

─❧❧─

virtually untrod paths to arrive at some promised land—for example, the giving of the Great Commission. Like those old movies, the Jesus stories all seem to have good endings.

Obviously Jesus's life was more than gripping stories with good endings. Perhaps it's this reminder: This Jesus God/man lived what he preached. I know, I know: for the sake of those he loved he was martyred at a relatively young age, but his way of approaching life—distinctly simple at its core and in its practice—has worked for those of us whose Conestoga wagons have followed the trail he first blazed.

I keep a big picture of Jesus in my office. It shows a tousled-hair guy with a friendly smile on his lips and in his eyes. He looks like someone who just finished diapering the baby for the umpteenth time, washing the dishes, playing touch football, chopping wood for the night's cooking, or teaching confirmation class. When I look at that painting, I am struck over and over again with this thought, as though a text message from Jesus to Bob, "No matter what UR facing, I've been there B4U."

When it comes to living simply, you can take a lot of comfort from knowing that what Jesus said about lifestyle—"Take no thought for tomorrow . . ."—was proven practical by what Jesus did with his life. The comfort comes in knowing that you can get clues for your decisions or difficult times from what Jesus said and did. You neither have to make up things as you go along nor pretend that in some Godlike way you can power your way out of troubles or confusion.

～✺～

Make a list of all the things in your home that need fixing. Next to each item write your feelings about the item and the cost (time and money) for the repair. What's the simplest way to deal with your feelings and the costs of repair?

～✺～

You Can Sustain What You Manage

I am hoping to live for three-score-and-ten years, plus a few more. (I sometimes half-jokingly tell people that my mission in life is to finish the Reformation, so I need all the time I can get.) That's why it's important for me to consider how long I can keep doing what's good or important. Over the several decades of my life so far, I have seen too many good ideas, programs, and people burned out, trashed, or dissed because they weren't manageable. I have also seen the frustration of leaders in the church trying to sustain unmanageable roles or ministries as though that task was the major requirement of their calling. That's why I wrote *Not Trying Too Hard: New Basics for Sustainable Congregations* (Alban Institute, 2001). I wanted church leaders to understand a biological truth that also fits congregations: If a living system manages its situation, it can continue to live over time.

The same dynamics can apply to you personally. This familiar example might suffice: If you continue to add things to your life—another car, a spiffy new rolling briefcase, that new five-blade razor, an energy-efficient refrigerator—you will eventually spend more and more time and money fixing those things. Because both time and money are limited commodities, what is used in one place cannot be used in another. Eventually you will reach the point where your life will become more and more complicated as you try to live with broken things or buy new things to replace the broken ones. The solution to this whole chain of cause and effect: possess fewer things.

How does manageability relate to sustainability? An unmanageable existence is by its very nature filled with stress. Stress is not a good thing for any of the systems of your body and soul, gradually tearing down organs, processes, identities, or outlooks on life. To say that in a positive way, if you are not stressed with continuing unmanageability, the systems of your body and soul will likely last longer, thus affording you the chance to sustain what you hope will be a productive and enjoyable life. That's pretty hopeful for the long run, don't you think?

And wouldn't you like to join me in finishing the Reformation?

You Want Simple Living to Be Fun

From personal experience, I have to tell you that simple-living folks really do live full and enjoyable lives. Once they get beyond thinking about simplicity as a set of techniques, simple-living adherents find that a lifestyle that is rich with possibilities.

To say that another way: when you are desperately living a life that you know just isn't working—or that requires every ounce of your energy to prop up or keep running—simplicity can look and feel very appealing, even fun. Not boring at all. Why? Because it doesn't require you to work two jobs, sentence your children to eternally traveling sports teams, or live off the second mortgage of a house whose net worth has now diminished by 20 percent.

To enjoy life to its fullest, you have to pay full attention to its wonders, beauties, and benefits. Otherwise, even an enjoyable life passes like a passenger train on a rainy night—you hear the sound but you are not on board. But when you slow down and deflate a lifestyle that's overstuffed and overrated, you find more capacity to pay attention to what really matters. That's an enjoyable, full, and fulfilling life!

The Gospel Encourages Your Simple Living

I have said this in several different ways in other chapters, but let me say it again here: The good news of God in Christ Jesus is part

⧽⧼

Read the obituaries—or Death Notices—in your local newspaper. What do you learn from these summaries of lives that were well-lived? Use what you read to frame the rest of your day or the content of your prayers.

⧽⧼

of the wider goodness of God's gracious rescue of humankind. When you are not afraid of death or growing older, when you are not trying to earn your way into others' favor, when you are really content about your life, when you have a just cause on which to center your life's meaning, and when you are protected by love wherever you go—in these circumstances the goodness of God shatters difficulty or evil like the light of a small, warm campfire in a cold wilderness night.

Profound enough to spread into every facet of life, God's good news enters your life as courage, love, grace, forgiveness, hope, or satisfaction. Because of the Spirit's other gifts—you know the list, right?—you have a reasonable assurance that you can live simply.

You Will Eventually Get There from Here

Simple living is a direction, not a destination. Because you can't describe the end result of "enough" very well in millimeters, milliliters, or milliseconds—or any other measurement known to humankind—you also can't measure your movement along some imagined path or trajectory. Instead you sense that simplicity is "over there" or "in that direction." And that's good enough.

Whenever I travel, I first check a map to get an overall feel for the geography of the place where I will spend some time. On arrival, I look around for landmarks, weather patterns, easily observed arteries of human commerce, the sun's path, or the direction in which local fleas hop—okay, maybe I made up that last one.

~~~

*Estimated amount of money spent in the United States each
year to treat ACL injuries in dogs: $1,320,000,000.*
—Vicki L. Wilke, Iowa State University, Ames
Reported in "Harper's Index," Harper's Magazine, *February
2006*

~~~

This helps when I try to find my way around, or if I am asked for directions. My automatic thought or answer is something like that of a dog—if dogs could talk: "It's over there." I adjust my position relative to "over there" and immediately know the general direction in which I will move or direct others' travel.

For me, simple living provides that same way of orienting myself to my context and having a general sense of the direction in which I am going. Instead of "southwest by west" or "Two blocks over and a couple of miles to the left," I might think of the direction as "Saying no for a while" or "Checking out the resale shop."

Knowing the direction without being able to name the exact destination or measure the way towards it is an almost-mystical experience. Once you move toward "over there," your first stop along the way tells you what's next. So "Saying no for a while" might remind you about "Do only what's truly important," and "Checking out the resale shop" might tell you to give away some of your clothes so you don't have to buy closet-organizing hardware, watch the newest "How to Organize Your Pitiful Life" DVD, or hire a full-time decluttering consultant.

You Want to Be Forgiven

Forgiveness is free, even for those of us who don't seek simplicity as we want or ought to. I love to wallow in God's grace and the forgiveness of others. Both are useful for me to remember when the barriers to simplicity rise up like those little cartoon monsters

⤙⤚

*Marketers are using MRI (magnetic resonance imaging) tests
to determine what's happening inside folks' brains when they
encounter product advertising. The scientists and advertisers
call this "neuromarketing." It's here to stay.*

⤙⤚

on television. (They are the creatures in television commercials
that sell remedies for everything from foot fungus to marauding
insects in your home.) The obstacles to simple living point scrawny
fingers at you and croak dangerous warnings. You might believe
them, especially when they gang up like the cartoon commercials
depict.

But forgiveness dispels the monstrous idea that you are only a
sinner beyond redemption. It gets you past trying to figure out how
you will save yourself and work your way into favored, simplicity
righteousness. Without deserving it, you receive—from God and
from others—assurance that your sinful actions and nonactions
are not the end of the story, that the monsters can be dispelled or
dissolved, that the cartoon story is not your life story.

So hear this personally: you are forgiven, friend. For every sin
you commit against this planet by your profligate possessing, for
every excuse you use to delay living joyfully, for every hurried day
during which you forget God and other people, God forgives you.
And if you and I know each other, I forgive you, too.

There! Do you see the monsters run away? And will you shut
off the television now?

You Are Living Simply for Good Reasons

On many days, I am powered past many of the barriers to simplicity by the simple question, "Why are you doing this, Bob?"
And I require of myself that the answer begin with the prompt,

"So that . . ." This mantra also works to keep me purposed and poised for action.

Where did I get the idea? John 3:16-17. There God's love is seen in God's intent for the world, for the people of the world. "For God *so* loved the world *that* he gave his only Son, *so that* . . ." (NRSV, italics added) presents a God who is always thinking, always moving, always looking around to see what needs to get done.

"So that . . ." motivates because it connects you to your life purpose. If you buy the proposition that your life is not your own and that you are trying to live out God's will for the world wherever you are, then you are motivated to find what's useful about everything around you and inside of you. When you want to make a difference, you look at your context and think, "Hey, how could this help me do what's right or necessary?" (Yes, this is another way of describing asset-based thinking.)

You Know You're Not the Only One Doing This

Before you and I head for the next chapter—watching these ideas in action—let me tell you what I think may be the most powerful antidote against the attitudes or beliefs that may thwart your desire or capability to live simply. It's another simple truth you already know: you are surrounded.

You are part of the body of Christ, and therefore you are intermeshed with entire systems of support and encouragement. Sometimes you are inside a cloud of witnesses described in Hebrews 12:1; at other times you are moving among a company of prophets like the one of which Elijah was a part. If you are fortunate, you may feel like you are part of the parade of worshipers depicted in Revelation. You are still buoyed up by others even if you think you are only part of a straggly band of followers who lost a little of their courage when their leader left.

Because you are not alone in this work of simple living, you can come out from the place where you are hiding, the desperate loneliness of thinking that you are the only one who yearns for

*Loneliness and the feeling of being unwanted is the most ter-
rible poverty.*
—Attributed to Mother Teresa

a manageable, just lifestyle. And you can invite others to do the
same.

You Can Stop Holding on Now

In this chapter you have considered how you might face barriers
that could deter you from moving in the direction of simplicity.
And you have also seen how God has provided some wonderful
defenses against those difficulties. You are ready now for what
comes next: Becoming part of an imagined group of people talking about simple living.

Now the fun begins.

Stop for a Moment

Fold a piece of paper in half, lengthwise. On the left-hand
column write all the subhead sentences in this chapter
that describe barriers and temptations. On the right-hand
column copy the "barrier buster" subhead sentences. See
which sentences motivate you, which satisfy you, which
agitate something inside you. How are you challenged,
comforted, or delighted? Which parts of your life connect
with the sentences?

4

How Will We Ever Change?

〜✦〜

P
eople don't just change by themselves. Or do they? Finding
the answer to that question is one of the Holy Grails of
congregational life. One school of thought—the Plan Your
Work and Work Your Plan crowd—would claim that the agency of
congregational leaders, especially clergy, is the key element in the
transformation of aimless wanderers into purposed disciples. Another school of thought—the Self-Ordering Chaos crew—proposes
that congregations organize their work according to seemingly
chaotic principles that congregation members value highly.

Both ideas have merit, certainly, but in this book I have been
advocating that second approach to change, trusting the power of
personal relationships embedded in earnest conversations about
what is truly important. By my reckoning, lifestyle change is *not*
going to happen within the lives of individuals and families because
a congregational committee somehow motivates them to examine
their most deeply held values and leads them gently toward new
ways of thinking and behaving. That might work with building
programs, Sunday school curricula, new ways of worshiping, or
congregational name-changing. But lifestyle patterns are much
more resistant to change when they are imposed from the outside.
If anyone wants to live more simply, justly, or joyfully, the person
makes that decision based on a host of factors—many of them
outside of the purview of the congregation—and then lives out
the decision, largely outside of the congregation's view.

You can lead a horse to water but you can't make it drink.
—Various sources

When it comes to changing lifestyle, the best any of us can do is to walk alongside beloved friends during the process of change.

One Year of Change

In the pages that follow, I introduce you to Pat, an individual committed to helping congregation members of Hope Church move from rushed and consumptive lifestyles to joyful, simple, and just ways of daily living. In this chapter you will follow Pat through one year of conversations about simple living, in a group Pat calls "Grandma's Gabbers." The chapter's narrative is contained in the artifacts of Pat's work, which invite you to imagine yourself into Pat's thoughts, words, and actions.

Pat and Hope Church are an amalgam of several of the thrilling people and situations I have encountered during my years of ministry. Sometimes prospering, sometimes just bumping along in their leadership roles, these people have led congregations in new ways and into new places regarding simplicity. As far as I know, they are still out there somewhere—California, Illinois, Texas, Pennsylvania—making simple living approachable and useful for the people they love. I hope the same for you.

To-Do List

September 3

* Find a quiet place to have coffee or breakfast with folks.
* Check my list of people I've noticed; invite them all personally.
* Check out who is out of work right now.
* Look around for who is stressed so badly that it shows.
* Read Wheatley's <u>Turning to One Another</u> again.
* Call up Garza and Liz; they seem to get the idea. (Both talked to me about working too hard, running too fast.)

*This is something I really want to do.
*Finding "just the right people" is an art.

Notes, First Conversation

1. Five of us found time on Saturday morning early, breakfast at Grandma Sally's Breakfast Barn (back room): Glenn Garza (computer guy); Elizabeth Blindt (single mother; son graduating from college next year); Frank and Mary (young couple I just met, different last names I didn't catch); me.
2. Explained why I invited them; we introduced each other and said a little about why we said yes. Was surprised how each of them told about feeling like they were completely different than people around them, maybe even odd.
3. We just talked about our experiences; didn't decide to do anything significant.
4. Agreed to talk early next month, same place and time. Grandma's has a good back room, quiet that time of day.

*Lots of small breakfast conversational groups at Grandma's; seemed to be from other churches—not just Bible study groups.

MY JOURNAL

September 14

These are the kind of people I <u>knew</u> we had in our church. How long it's been since I've talked to anyone who understands—or cares about—living simply. It's like I've crossed the desert and found a spring-fed stream to drink from. I could learn from these people, and I think they want to keep talking together. I have to read that Margaret Wheatley book again, so I don't turn this group into a team or a committee. Or get forced into keeping minutes or a report. I probably should tell Pastor that a few of us are getting together to talk about simple living—it seems like the right thing to do. I think the group wants me to be the Conversation Starter.

WHILE YOU WERE OUT

September 22

Pat:

Mr. Glenn Garza called today; he will be unable to keep his Saturday morning breakfast appointment with you. Call him at his cell phone (885.555.0067). That's where he can be reached while he's traveling the next three weeks.

WHILE YOU WERE OUT

September 29

Pat:
Ms. Blindt—says she knows you—wants you to
call her back. Something about a breakfast group
and a friend of hers. Call evenings—after 8:00 PM
at 555.0014.

*Liz has lots of friends like her.

From the Pastor's Desk

September 30

Pat!

Thanks for your phone message last Sunday evening.
Sorry I missed you. Yes, I'd be interested in knowing
more about the breakfast conversation group you've put
together, and, yes, I understand your concern about
forming another committee at church. Let's talk some-
time to see if I can be helpful. Or just e-mail me at hope@
downcast.net.

Pastor Casey

From: pat0942@atttt.net
Sent: October 3
To: hope@downcast.net

Pastor Casey:

Thanks for your note and for the brief conversation before Sunday school last week. You're right: "Conversation about lifestyle" is a good way to describe what we're going to be doing. And I agree that the group could probably get larger over time, especially if we make a note of it in an article in our *Hope Is Happening* e-newsletter. But let's hold off on that for now, okay? I'm still trying to get my head around a group that doesn't have an official place in the congregation, doesn't get anything done, but is very important for almost every member of our congregation. Strange, hmm?

Here's what I propose: If you hear of individuals who are really wrestling with the way they're living—or you just get the sense that their lives are out of control—give me their names and what you can share about them without breaking confidence. Perhaps over time we can expand our little coffee klatch into something a little bigger. For now, the conversation needs to get on a solid footing.

BTW, if you need to call us by a name, we joked about Grandma's Gabbers. Does that work for you?

Pat

*Should I have told Pastor more than this? Or is this too much?

Notes to Self

October 15

* Garza couldn't come again on Saturday, but wants to continue the conversation.
* He volunteered to see if he could get us hooked together in some Web meeting software thing. Not sure, so I said sure.
* Elizabeth Blindt has a friend she wants to bring along next time. The group said okay, but I'm not sure.
* Do we need topics next time—maybe Saturday's newspaper—or just wing it?
* The young couple turned out to be real radicals—maybe vegans or environmental activists. They work in some nonprofit that promotes urban gardening and locally grown food. I'm glad they're here.
* Pastor Casey wants to drop in some of the time. Group said yes; seemed happy about the validation. Maybe we can help with sermons?

MY JOURNAL

November 20

The Grandma's Gabbers got together for the second and third conversations, and it's going well. We're up to six or seven—depending whether Glenn comes. Frank and Mary (von Kledell and Haupreiter are their last names) keep bringing two folks from their work. Elizabeth's friend came once and didn't come back; she needs a support group.

Sure, we'll support each other, but real support groups have a different purpose than ours.

Pastor Casey has been very helpful. Sometimes the discussion gets a little too deep with Pastor around, but I think it keeps people from being negative. Some of this simple living stuff connects with our church's hunger and justice work. Puts us on a path wider than just preserving the environment or taking care of ourselves. Gets us thinking about Jesus, the Bible, what God wants—that sort of thing.

No other referrals yet, though, for any new Gabbers.

I'm not sure what folks are getting out of the group. I wrestle with the feeling that we should be doing something—like building a Habitat house together, or writing our congressperson or putting articles online in *Hope Is Happening*. So far I'm not interested in doing that, and no one is actually pushing in that direction, so perhaps we're okay.

One thing I've noticed: the sharing is getting more personal—last week Mary talked about how her first husband's death was a wake-up call about life priorities that she didn't pay attention to. Glenn has opened up about how his work life is killing his personal life—and about how everyone at his company seems to be in the same boat. Good things to think about, for all of us.

Me? I'm just happy that we're still talking. And Grandma Sally's is happy for the business, too.

ORDER FORM

Barb's Books
November 30
8 copies *Voluntary Simplicity (Revised Edition)* by Duane Elgin

*Barb said that there are thousands of books on this subject. How could I possibly choose from among them?

From: pat0942@atttt.net
Sent: December 12
To: GLGarza@compucop.com; gardeners2@radicalfood.
org; aeblindt@sbsglobal.com; jennfarsi@commcast.net;
hope@downcast.net; bethfred02@redrivercomm.com

Hello to All:

Just a quick note to bring you up to speed on some of
the things we've been talking about:
1. Happy Advent to you all! What a great conversation about buying gifts for our families. (I'm trying the
Hunger Program special giving opportunities catalog.)
Mary and Beth: Your childhood memories were helpful
to us all.
2. Let's not meet on the 18th. Grandma Sally's is closing
for two weeks—"Grandma" is a skier—so our favorite
place won't be available. I'll get back to you about another date after the holidays.
3. Pastor Casey has asked whether some of us could
write the Christmas Eve services prayers—like you did
for the ecumenical Thanksgiving Service, Fred. Anyone
interested, let Pastor know.
4. I'm sorry I wasn't as focused in our conversation
earlier this month. Every so often it hits me that this
simplicity thing automatically makes me into a raving
hypocrite when I think about the forced simple living
that happens for poor people all over the world every
day. That thought was grabbing me and wouldn't let go;
that's why I was grumpy.
5. Jenn, sorry that we won't see you for a couple of
months. We understand how you have to take care

of your aging parents for a while now, and we'll miss you. Check in when you get back, okay? BTW, thanks for your wonderful chocolate chip cookies for each of us—something to remember you by.

6. Herb Frederking—the congregation president—wants to talk with us after the holidays about starting another one of these conversation groups. I put him off, but wanted you to think about this matter with me.

7. Elizabeth: Thanks for the heads-up about getting guest columns into the *StarGazer*. I always wondered how people could get their opinions into our local paper. I may follow up with the contact person you gave me. Maybe something about "a simple Christmas." Maybe one of your poems?

8. When we get back together, can we talk about something more than just money and things, hmmm? I get the feeling that it's *time use* that's toughest for all of us; maybe we've been avoiding the subject. Or it's just too hard to get a handle on.

See you after the holidays! And see you in church. Look for an e-mail after the holidays, about the date and place for our next conversation.

God keep you joyful!

Pat

P.S. Yes, the books are a gift to you from me.

> *How do we keep in contact over the holidays? Or should we just have a vacation for a while?

Pastor:

Some of us want to talk with you about the youth group's silent auction. Yes, we have some problems. Anytime's fine, maybe a breakfast this week.

Pat

*THIS is a big problem!

From: hope@downcast.org
Sent: January 4
To: pat0942@atp.net

Pat:

Thanks for the phone call. I'm sorry that I can't meet with your group this week. Maybe next week. Before we talk together, though, I have to tell you that I don't necessarily agree with your take on the silent auction in the Gathering Area on Sundays. And I hope that you don't bring our new youth director into the conversation quite yet.

Looking forward to breakfast. How about next Thursday? Grandma Sally's?

Pastor Casey

From: pat0942@atttt.net; aeblindt@sbsglobal.com
Sent: January 5
To: GLGarza@compucop.com; gardeners2@radicalfood.
org; jennfarsi@commcast.net; hope@downcast.net;
bethfred02@redrivercomm.com

To Grandma's Gabbers:

Pastor Casey has agreed to meet with us about the youth group's silent auction, and thought that maybe next Thursday would work. Let me know if you can make breakfast that morning, okay? In case you missed church or haven't been reading the news in *Hope Is Happening*, here's what I think occurred:

1. The youth leader wanted to galvanize the kids into action of some kind. She thought that a silent auction would help raise money for their ministries. She's new, so no one objected.
2. Someone else—our pastor?—arranged to start that DVD course on consumerism by the theologian Walter Brueggemann, FOR THE SAME SUNDAY as the silent auction. Did anyone else see the irony in this? Or the contradiction?
3. Elizabeth, after you and I talked at church on that Sunday, I sent Pastor Casey a note, and we talked briefly about this matter.
4. Pastor doesn't see any problem with the silent auction. I hope you do.

If you can come to breakfast, let me know here. I'll say yes to Pastor, on the strength that some of us can be present.

Thanks,
Pat

From: GLGarza@compucop.com
Sent: January 8
To: pat0942@atttt.net

Pat:

Can't make it that morning. Have to be in Portland for a meeting. If I could come, though, I'd agree with the pastor. You and Elizabeth may be seeing danger where there isn't any. What can it hurt for the kids to make some money for a good cause?

Glenn

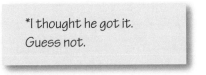

*I thought he got it.
Guess not.

From: gardeners2@radicalfood.org
Sent: January 7
To: pat0942@atttt.net

Pat:

We strongly agree with your concerns. We see a big contradiction between fighting consumerism while at the same time promoting the silent purchasing of stuff. (Does the silence make that kind of materialism some-how okay?) But we're not going to come to the break-fast. Why? We have enjoyed the conversations with all of you, but don't really want to get into congregational politics or programs. They're just not that important to us right now. Figuring out how to feed hungry people is. Thanks for understanding.

Frank and Mary

P.S. Fred and Beth won't be there, either. They don't agree with each other about simple living in the same way—she's a saver and he's a pitcher—and this additional conflict just wouldn't help their marriage. They probably won't answer your e-mail, either. You probably should have left them out of the e-mail group.

From: jennfarsi@commcast.net
Sent: January 7
To: pat0942@atttt.net; aeblindt@sbsglobal.net

Elizabeth and Pat:

Thanks for the invite. I won't be there—I'm not part of your church and my parents are very ill out West. I thought you knew that already. To be honest, it bothers me that you'd ask me to come talk about something that's really not all that important to the world I live in. Frankly, your note helped remind me why I'm not part of a church.

Jenn

From: pat0942@atttt.net
Sent: January 10
To: aeblindt@sbsglobal.net

Elizabeth:

It's you and me with Pastor Casey next Thursday, break-fast, Grandma Sally's. Everyone else has a problem with the date or the idea. We may have lost some of our crew over this one. Maybe we stepped over a line? I'm getting discouraged.

Pat

From: aeblindt@sbsglobal.net
Sent: January 11
To: pat0942@atttt.net

Pat:

I'll be there, with bells on. This is worth getting riled up about. Think of it: our own congregation, promoting simplicity out of one side of its mouth, and out of the other legitimating consumerist ways of funding mission. As in, "Buy something for a good cause." Reminds me of that star-studded Buy Red program awhile back. Like consumerism is okay as long as it raises money to do something good. Sad and wrong.

Elizabeth

> *Good old Liz. When it comes to simplicity, we're soul mates. Without her I'd run out of steam. And she's got plenty of it!

Meeting Notes

Grandma Sally's Breakfast Barn
Thursday, January 15
Present: Casey, Elizabeth, Pat

1. No agreement among the three of us. Pastor's okay with the auction, Elizabeth's frothing at the mouth, and I'm just bothered by the lack of thought by our congregational leadership.
2. Elizabeth's point: the church ought to live what it teaches. If consumerism isn't a good thing, then it makes no sense at all to pretend that silent-auction consumerism is generosity. I see the point, and I respect her anger, especially if we're being two-faced by offering that Brueggemann course.
3. The pastor's point: a greater good is at work here—the congregation getting behind the youth group's restart. We're condemning the baby for being in its bath water.
4. My dilemma: I don't agree with the pastor at all—that logic has a hole big enough to drive a truck through—but I can't get as riled up as Elizabeth.
5. No actions taken, no decisions made. We just talked.
6. Another obvious point: our conversation group probably fell apart during the Christmas break. Or maybe I'm wrong. How can I get the conversation going again?

MY JOURNAL

January 22

I think I ruined something good: people talking together about what's really important. There we were—getting to know each other, with no church program pressure—and I decided that we had to do something about a supposed congregational problem. I think I let go of the assets that I had in order to chase a problem that probably chewed up the people I value. Is this how it always happens in the church?

MY JOURNAL

February 2

Weird. It's like our group dropped off the edge of the world or turned into dust. No phone calls, no letters, no e-mails from anyone. I haven't spoken to Elizabeth or Pastor Casey since our breakfast meeting. I think Elizabeth may have stopped coming to church for a while. She really feels strongly about the whole hypocrisy thing—saying one thing and then doing another. Maybe when you feel strongly enough about simplicity you face down the hypocrites inside of you and outside of you. A frustrating place to be, caught between integrity and confession. Maybe we need to learn how to forgive each other. And ourselves . . .

To-Do List

Simple Living Group
February 15

1. Start over, a re-beginning? Talk with Eliza-
    beth first.
2. Be more patient this time. Trust conver-
    sation, not e-mail. Loosen up. The phone
    works.
3. Maybe start with a simple living book
    of some kind; something evocative, not
    preachy or burdened with handy hints.
4. Invite the former participants personally.
5. Tell the church council what we're doing, but
    don't ask for permission.

*This is tougher than I thought it would be; I'm not giving up, though.

WHILE YOU WERE OUT

February 19
10:35 a.m.

Pat:
Mr. Glenn Garza called from Minot. Hoped you
would remember him. Sounded excited. Will call
again at your home phone tonight.

WHILE YOU WERE OUT

February 19
10:50 a.m.

Pat:
Mr. Garza again. Wants to get more copies of the book you sent him last year. For his National Sales Manager and her family. Can you phone him back tonight at his Minot hotel number (701.555.0955) with the title?

WHILE YOU WERE OUT

February 19
1:24 p.m.

Garza again. Wants to know if you're still interested in Web conferencing for this group. He can get you a deal.

*What's this all about?

Inside Out
by Elizabeth Blindt

Another Spring?

The seasons move into and out of our lives. Now spring comes knocking, and in this month's column I want to offer you a few thoughts that I hope will add sparkle to this seasonal change. They have to do with the way you live.

Living Green

Spring is about green, and "living green" is what lots of folks around here are trying to do. In my church, for example, a group of people has started a community garden on the property. I know a man who travels way too much but manages to ask for organic food in every restaurant he frequents. (He's an account representative and knows about creating markets.) You might start thinking about how your lifestyle results in a light footstep on the Earth. A good place to begin: assess your ecological footprint at *www.ecofoot.org*. The results could surprise you.

Slowing Down

Spring comes slowly, the warmth creeping into our bones like a gentle hug from a dear friend. This season's dawning might be a good time to start thinking about the speed of your life or its complexity. A good beginning place: the online lifestyle survey at *www.simplelivingamerica.org/survey*. I know how hard it can be, but think about smelling the flowers this spring. Slowly.

Generosity

Spring reminds you of the amazing generosity of this planet toward its inhabitants. Life regenerates itself, in spite of our treatment of the environment. How amazing that this takes place at all. Your generosity—giving to causes that transcend your self-interest—is a good way to learn from Mother Nature during this time.

She did it. A regular column in the paper!

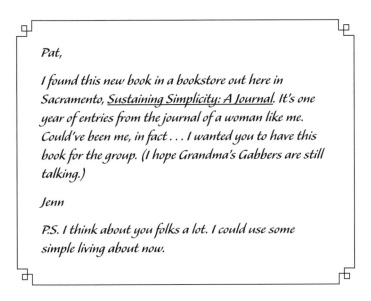

Pat,

I found this new book in a bookstore out here in Sacramento, <u>Sustaining Simplicity: A Journal</u>. It's one year of entries from the journal of a woman like me. Could've been me, in fact . . . I wanted you to have this book for the group. (I hope Grandma's Gabbers are still talking.)

Jenn

P.S. I think about you folks a lot. I could use some simple living about now.

From the Pastor's Desk

March 22

Pat:

Haven't talked with you or Liz for a while. You okay? Still meeting with your simplicity group? I hope so, because this past week or so a few more folks have surfaced in the congregation—and folks sort of connected to the congregation—who you might want to invite into your conversation. Here they are:

Me (and Blair, too)—I've been thinking about that Silent Auction flap a few months ago. On reflection, I see what you and Liz were talking about. The strangest thing: that day so many people went to the silent auction that only five members came to the consumerism course. "You can't serve two masters," Jesus said. I should've known . . .

Herb Frederking—He decided not to run for council president next year. Told me that he needs to sort out the clutter and slow down the pace of his life. I suggested a life coach, but he's not quite ready. You could help him at this stage in his life.

The Nessions—Paul and Belinda. He's national guard just back from Iraq and she's a stay-at-home mom who used to be a teacher. Two kids, school-age. The family's interested in Hope, but say they "don't need any church membership" stress right now. Your group's conversation could be helpful for either or both of them.

Adam Djovroak—(I think that's how you spell his name.) He's been visiting here for a while—from Eastern Europe, graduate school—and has talked to me about his interest in Christianity as a way of living. I think he has some theological training, or maybe he's studying sociology of religion.

I'll ask these people soon, or let Liz do some of the asking.

MY JOURNAL

April 2

What a fool I was. Just when it seemed nothing was happening, the seeds start growing again. Pastor Casey has introduced me to four new people at church, and three of the old group have agreed to come back. And Blair is coming, too!

We'll do things differently this time. (I'm not even sure what that means.) We'll start with the breakfasts and good conversation.

A List of Topics We Sort of Talked About

June 15

Over the past ten weeks, we've met four times and talked personally about these ideas. Sometimes briefly, sometimes deeply. I think they connect somehow, but not just yet . . .

* Global warming's effects right here, right now.
* The way Jesus lived—can it work these days?
* Who is influencing our kids to be greedy?
* How to say no in a positive and helpful way.
* People notice us when we live simply. (Or do they ignore us?)

* Glenn's idea that businesses need to live simply, too. (Yes, he's back!)
* Where is the Bible in all this?
* How odd it is to be pushed around by the presumptions of the marketplace.
* The silliness of so much of the advertising we see. Like everyone's dumb.
* Trash and junk. (We talked about this twice.)
* How living simply can destroy a marriage, or make it stronger.
* Slowing down Elizabeth's schedule. (It was like a case study, but she was okay with it.)
* The small simplicities.
* What does simplicity feel like if you're poor?
* What keeps any of us from living a truly simple life?
* The news of the week. Every week.
* What to pray about? Who to pray for?

Strange thing: One of the waitresses at Grandma's seems to be listening in bits and pieces. She asked me some good questions after our last breakfast. I'm inviting her to the Sunday picnic we set for the end of July.

I wonder if any of this seems silly to anyone except us.

From the Pastor's Desk

June 20

Pat:

I'm glad you decided to continue the conversation group over the summer. Grandma's Gabbers has become a necessary feature of my life, and I sense that the times we get together have made a difference for all the people who come, whenever they can make it.

I hope you've noticed that being in the group has helped me with my sermon emphases—lots of the texts in the lectionary can be interpreted through a simplicity filter. I have also noticed in my counseling that over and over again what's eating at people—especially couples—are their mistaken presumptions about "the good life." I'm thinking of asking the council to investigate how we could include life coaching as a ministry of this congregation. Maybe partially support a center or a coach for our folks?

I'm also excited that the stewardship team has taken up lifestyle as a topic for consideration during our annual funding appeal this fall. They've come to see what you probably already knew: people living too fast on credit don't really have anything to give to the ministries of this congregation. Time or money. "Abundant Life" might be the theme for the fall program.

From the Pastor's Desk

Anyhow, this long letter is my way of saying thanks for what you've started at Hope. I look forward to seeing how Grandma's Gabbers continues to flourish, to make a difference in people's lives, and to helping each of us make sense out of our callings in life. (And no, we won't be making this into a program of the congregation. You're doing just fine without that.)

Pastor Casey

P.S. Blair and I both have come to realize that our marriage can't continue without our purposely slimming down our waistlines, de-stuffing our home, slowing down our pace, and learning to say no. It was a tough conversation, but we came to see that we just couldn't keep going on like before. Thanks for helping our family prosper in a new way.

MY JOURNAL

August 23

Almost a year now. And the conversations continue. Not much seems to come of them, but I get the sense that something's bubbling under the surface, like a simmering stew. People keep coming back, and I know that they must certainly talk with other folks—where they work, at home, at church. Maybe this idea has to stay invisible to spread. Its power—people gaining courage from each other— works no matter whether visible or invisible.

I'm not sure about this, but I think some other people may be having the same conversations with their friends. I overheard our youth director talking with some parents about teens working for money to buy things they don't need. That's a good sign. I still hope we don't ever make these groups into a formal program. It would be good enough if our conversations were like good bacteria in the congregation's digestive tract!

I'd be satisfied with that.

*Can any of us ever be satisfied with our simplicity?
*What does "simple enough" mean for me?

Looking Back

Grandma's Gabbers may be an imagined group, but its potential in your life—as an example for your own conversations—may be great. To help develop that prospect, follow me as I go back through Pat's year and offer these observations about what took place.

The Flow

Groups develop according to predictable patterns. Cycles of growth and decline are natural for any group, each part of the cycle being caused by and causing another part of the cycle. The Gabbers in this chapter would likely have floundered several more times during the year, at least in small ways. But as a wise leader, Pat would have resisted the temptation to analyze too closely each relational hiccup or bump in the road. Over time, hiccups disappear and roads level out; the same is true with conversational groups. Unlike groups purposed by a task or outcome, conversational groups are measured by one standard: that their members keep talking with each other, honestly and earnestly.

Mistakes

In concert with Elizabeth, Pat made several errors that almost torpedoed the group. Some were obvious—tangling with the pastor—and some not as easily seen—overwrought memos. Friendships allow for these miscues, though, because the promise of an energizing exchange of thoughts and emotions most likely pulls conversational compatriots towards their next encounter. Too many problems, of course, may indicate that the premises on which the group is based are shaky or that the conversations need to go to a deeper level. With Grandma's Gabbers, the energy of conversation kept flowing around the mistakes.

～✥～

One way to find lifestyle leaders in your congregation: With other members, host simplicity conversations in your homes. Over time you'll find out who's working on simple living, even if only in small ways. Tell your host(s) what you've noticed, and what you appreciate about their lifestyle.

～✥～

Group Composition

Like many informal groups, Grandma's Gabbers formed in ways that defy easy analysis. No personality profiles were assembled, no checklists of requirements for group membership developed, no quota system devised to assure diversity, no nominations or voting. Pat used native intuition, some luck, and the referrals of others to form and maintain the group's membership. Perhaps that's enough.

Subtleties

Although I painted this group's portrait with a broad brush, you probably picked up—or added—subtle ideas, emotions, or directions. In some ways, the subtle benefits of conversation are the most important features of this type of social change.

Why is that? Subtleties require many different brain structures to work together cleverly as they search for the meaning or patterns in what is understated, faint, or seemingly chaotic. Brain structures like to work together—neuroscientists call this "whole brain" activity—and so enjoy the prospect of humor, puzzles, flirting, any artistic endeavor, or conversations. Conversations both hide and reveal the subtleties of relationships. So what nuances did you pick up, what finer points of group interaction?

~≈~

*I would not give a fig for the simplicity this side of complexity,
but I would give my life for the simplicity on the other side of
complexity.*
—*Attributed to Oliver Wendell Holmes Jr.*

~≈~

The Pastor

Why did I put Pastor Casey—and spouse Blair—into the group? It's hard for clergy and their families to participate with others in intimate, enjoyable conversation free from the constraints of their professional roles as leaders or helpers. Simple living—read "managing a schedule"—is especially difficult for pastors and their families, if only because this is a profession frequently without an OFF DUTY sign. Inserting the pastor into Grandma's Gabbers suggests that principled conversations about simple living might bring value to a pastor you know and love.

Artifacts

One good way to observe behaviors is to look at the trail of artifacts that results from those behaviors. In this chapter those artifacts were confined to the limits of the printed page, but in real life the artifacts of conversations might include objects of any kind.

Why pay attention to artifacts? As bearers of evidence of meaningful behaviors, artifacts can show what people value or don't value. Artifacts are good conversation starters, too. They serve as memory recall devices or reminders for gratitude or prayer. Perhaps the greatest value of artifacts: they invoke imagination, asking observers, users, or handlers to reconstruct the behavior or value that resulted in the artifact. So a handmade clay pot on my desk might remind me of the person who gave it to me and

~≈~

*Buy a frame, a small tabletop pedestal, or a square of beautiful
fabric. Use any of these items to highlight or set apart some ordinary or simple artifact of your life in a visible location. Keep it
there for a week, then change the featured object. After a month,
see what's changed with your thinking about "ordinary."*

~≈~

the valuable insights this person freely shared with me. Or a water
bottle from a conference might help me recall the conference's
experiences.

Conversation Content

Because conversations are good examples of self-ordering social
systems, it was important to Pat that the Gabbers group didn't fall
into predictable present-and-discuss or interview formats. These
modes of interaction are usually not random, spontaneous, or
freewheeling. Each is rooted in the presumption that the topical
content of the conversation is the sole key to its success. To keep
conversation times from turning into classes or workshops, Pat
guided conversation away from overpurposed and impersonal
discussions of ideas. Pat also helped each conversant speak freely
and honestly, no matter what the content.

Lasting and Changing

It's hard to say how many more years Grandma's Gabbers will
last, given the general character of small groups. The composi-
tion of the group may change, its frequency of meetings vary, or
its connection to the congregation evolve. But because the group
started on a good footing, it has a good chance of outlasting most

※⚮※

*Talk about what you yearn for, or what's good, true, or beauti-
ful about your life. What's not working very well? What, really,
compels you to live the way you do?*

※⚮※

congregational programs and even the individuals who started
the group. Not bound or motivated by the responsibility of your
congregation's institutional health or governance, this group will
likely continue to be energized by mutual appreciation, growing
capacities, and emotional honesty.

If you look closely around your community, you may find a
de facto group just like the one in this chapter, quietly equipping
its on-and-off-again members to live wisely in a world somehow
bent toward foolishness.

Where to look? Any early morning diner or coffee shop with
the word *Grandma* in its name.

5

Could We Talk?

After sending many words in your direction, I would love the chance to sit down with you—for lunch, I think—and hear some words coming from you. We would chat about this subject, of course, but, perhaps more important, also about what you might be doing to simplify your life.

I think the lunch would be fun, if only because I would learn how much you already know, how simply you already live. Maybe how deeply you think about this subject or how fully you have integrated simplicity into your life goals. It would be enjoyable to meet you and start our own conversation. Especially if your name were Pat.

In this chapter, I am going to move in that direction, thinking of these pages as my part of our conversation about how to talk with others about simple living. Imagine us at lunch—I favor salads or Reuben sandwiches—with this subject on our minds, each of us excited about the prospect of connecting with others for whom simple living is a core issue.

It will be a good lunch.

How It All Starts

In my experience, most important changes begin with two people talking about something that necessarily strikes both of them as important. Sometimes the first encounter is planned, but most of

Lifework—the job title they'll put on your headstone.

the time it's not. Here's how I think this change process works: You are talking with someone whom you just met or someone you just like to talk with. One of you hears a comment that gives you permission to head down the conversational pathway called "simple living." The conversation suddenly coalesces around that subject for a moment or two before moving along to something else. But in the moments during which simplicity is at the center of attention, you come to know that other person as someone with whom you can trust the sometimes-private matters of your attempts at simple living. The rest, as they say, is history.

Like you, I have been present at these first conversations, the backs-and-forths that draw people together into some larger purpose or identity. Let me tell you about several of these starter conversations.

Once in a church basement I met a couple—former missionaries—who are living a very full life on a very small income in a very small home in a very small town in North Dakota. We talked for a long time about their practice of simple living. I told them I wished that more people around the country could meet them. They stopped my gushing with a respectful reminder: if they started doing workshops and making presentations everywhere, they would have to give up their simple lives. That's when I first learned how the most principled simplicity is probably the hardest to see.

A few years ago I happened upon a new coworker. Our conversation started with an odd greeting, "How come I haven't met you before?" Simple living came into the conversation when I asked how this person could make a living with only a part-time job at our place of work. Over time others joined in the conversation; this larger group of people eventually helped renew our denomination's simple-living emphasis. Think of it: an offbeat conversation-starter

❦

No person is your friend (or kin) who demands your silence, or
denies your right to grow.
—Attributed to Alice Walker

❦

helped reshape the program by which an entire church body approaches this subject.

Perhaps most gratifying have been my late-night conversations with some of the guests at the homeless shelter where I volunteer. When I get beyond my unhelpful pitying of these folks, I ask more respectful questions about their lives. One question always elicits answers that help me remember what's important; I ask, "What's ahead for you this week?" From the guests' frank and poignant responses I have culled this summary life-axiom: do first what's first important; the rest can wait.

Relationships start with one-on-one conversations that continue to grow because of very simple clues. Sometimes the clues are just a word or a phrase, at other times a hint of body language or facial expression. When I meet someone new or get the chance to talk intimately with someone I have known for a while, I listen for conversation appetizers about simplicity. I think of these moments as the seeds of a new or deeper friendship or perhaps even the time when some important change might begin.

❦

Stop for a Moment

Close your eyes and rewind the mental video of your week thus far. Now think about the most meaningful, rewarding, or helpful conversation in which you engaged this week. When during the conversation did you know it was going to be a good one? How did you know that? What few words, phrases, actions, or facial expressions did you notice? Now open your eyes and keep reading to see how you and I share similar experiences.

~≈~

What to Listen For

Sometimes I hear a few words and phrases that tell me when I'm with folks who might just be ready for a deeper, longer conversation about their need to change the way they live. Their words might sound like these:

- I'd love to meet someone who knows how to say no.
- I don't know what to do with my kids.
- I'm always tired.
- I'd slow down if I could.
- My calendar? Let me check my kids' schedule first.
- We never have time for each other anymore.
- We just can't keep living this way for much longer.
- Most of the time I don't have time.
- We have more stuff than we know what to do with.
- If I was honest, I'd admit that my life is basically out of control.
- If quiet were for sale, I'd buy some, if I had some money.
- I'm ready to give up trying.
- Things used to be more fun.

People who have been working at this matter for a while are also around you. Their language also helps identify them. They say things like this:

- We've started cutting back on Christmas gifts.
- It's about time we started being honest about obesity.

Some of my colleagues live on slow clocks—they come late to meetings, miss deadlines, get to things when they can, and talk a lot together. I think they enjoy their work in a different way than I do. I admire them.

- I really don't care what other people think about the way I dress.
- The less I do, the more I have fun doing it.
- We cut up all of our credit cards except two.
- I think we have something to learn from people we call "poor."
- Multitasking? It's a lie.
- My cell phone is already turned off.
- I think I know why the environment is going to hell in a handbasket.
- We have mostly stopped watching television.
- Want to have some *real* fun?
- We're thinking of living on one salary for a while.
- I've started walking more; it feels great.
- I don't mind waiting.
- We eat together a lot more than we used to.
- The two of us are spending more time together now.
- We've told the grandparents, "No more toys!"
- We're retiring right here.
- Does anyone else think *happy* is different than *joyful*?

What Happens Next

When I hear people sharing word-clues about simplicity, I'm excited. I know that these are like-minded individuals with whom the conversation can continue, whether they are thinking about

*Dedicate one part of a room, your office, or your car as a sim-
plicity sanctuary, a place where you can sit, stand, or rest free of
harried schedules, unreasonable demands, excess stuff, or noise.
Spend time there each day.*

moving toward simpler living or already living that way. I follow
their comments or questions with some appreciative responses
that help them talk even more openly about their thoughts,
questions, or feelings. Here are some ways I might continue the
conversations:

- How did you figure that out?
- Why's that important to you?
- I can see how you might think that way.
- How long have you been thinking about this?
- How's that idea (practice) working out for you?
- I know what you're saying; a lot of us are thinking the
  same way.
- I hope you don't think that you're all alone in thinking
  this way.
- It's tough, I know.
- How do you know that's true (that will work)?
- What would you say if I invited you to gather with a group
  of people at church who have been talking about these
  subjects for a while now and who would welcome you into
  their happy fellowship next Sunday night for supper—and
  could you bring some lime Jell-O? (Actually, I don't usually continue any beginning conversation with an invitation
  to "come on down to church." That's for later, perhaps
  much later.)

~≈~

Avoiding danger is no safer in the long run than outright exposure. The fearful are caught as often as the bold.
—Helen Keller

~≈~

Sometimes the Oddball

Sometimes it's okay to try out some unorthodox conversational gambits—and to risk being misunderstood, resisted, or ignored—in order to shake a verbal exchange loose from its "let's all be nice" loops. I remember one writer's workshop when I was working with an aspiring writer who wanted to write deeply about spirituality in her small town. After a careful reading of the imposing edifices this writer had constructed out of gushy, platitude-filled prose, I invited her back for a check-in conversation. I looked at her, thought a second about where to start talking, then blurted out, "What are you trying to hide?" Tears and honesty tumbled out, as did her confessions about feeling disregarded as a pastor's spouse. She dearly wanted her writing to help other pastors' sometimes-invisible wives find their strengths and capabilities. So I followed my first cheeky question with a kinder one, "Why don't you write about what you just told me?" Less than an hour later she came back with a devotional piece that was emotionally rich, devoid of churchy verbosity, and potentially helpful to pastors and their spouses. I have wondered since then whether she is still writing in such an evocative and inviting way. I hope so.

Impertinence may not be your style—it has its problems, as my few remaining friends would tell you—but perhaps you could bring a conversation to a deeper, or at least different, level with follow-up questions or comments like these:

Talk with someone who is obese about the reasons for their condition, their feelings about their bodies, and their opinions about others' opinions. Why do so many people continue to carry around dangerous extra pounds, and why do so many people look down on them?

- Are you sure about what you're saying? Why?
- What are you looking for?
- So where do you think all this (the things you've just said) is leading you?
- I don't understand what you're saying; use some different words.
- How are things working out for you?
- What's preventing you from doing what you say you really want to do?
- We have only these few minutes to talk; let's talk about what's most important to you.
- Stop telling me about feeling guilty; tell me how you are already living simply.
- Why are you telling me all this?
- What are you trying to hide?

When I use these unusual methods to move a conversation toward a deeper level, I take comfort from the story of Jesus's treatment of the Syrophoenician woman who told Jesus that "even dogs eat the crumbs that children drop from the table" (Mark 7:28). I admire the ways this very wise woman turned Jesus's possible impertinence into an important conversation with good results for her child *and* for Jesus. I think of his conversations with Pharisees, Pilate, his disciples—how those exchanges sometimes began with impolite or even brazen violations of genteel conversational norms.

Jesus knew how to cut to the core of a conversation, right away and usually with good results.

Even though I am basically a shy fellow, I continue to use these unconventional conversational strategies from time to time. Three reasons come to mind: (1) This method usually allows or encourages an exchange that's more emotionally honest; (2) most of the time people push back at me, which immediately establishes their ownership of the conversation and helps them understand that I am also a learner; (3) we get to what's important before we run out of time.

Stop for a Moment

I'm willing to risk seeming like a jerk—or being one temporarily—to engage in rewarding conversations. If this approach doesn't work for you or fit your preferred conversational styles, spend a moment right now thinking about your natural skills as a participant in conversations. Whatever your preferred style of conversation, write down four adjectives or adverbs that characterize its strengths. Keep that slip of paper in your wallet or purse. Or in the doggie bag from our lunch.

What Keeps a Simplicity Conversation Going

My experience is that, once started, conversations about simple living travel farther and deeper than most conversations. The reasons? Perhaps it's the nature of the subject that bonds people in mutual appreciation. Or perhaps lifestyle conversations naturally

---

The right word at the right time is like precious gold set in silver.
—*Proverbs 25:11*

---

occur in an atmosphere already filled with common understanding, common curiosity, or common needs.

Having said that, I can think of some pointers that might help you continue your simple-living conversations past their first delightful exchanges. These are the awkward moments when you have taken a strand of conversation to its logical end and you are not sure where to go next—even though you know that oodles of curiosities and similarities are yet to be explored. (Somewhere in my dusty past I have read that observers of interpersonal conversation—hereafter called "they" to denote their authority as experts—call these moments "conversational lags" and that these pauses occur about 20 minutes after the conversation begins.)

Here are some suggestions for you to consider as you have conversations that last for a while:

1. Review what you already know about helpful listening skills and attitudes. A conversation is not a soliloquy, an interview, or a sales pitch. You honor the other conversant with your silence as well as your words. Good questions offer as much value as good statements.

2. Stories work. Unless they are protracted and convoluted—and use big words like *protracted* and *convoluted*—narratives of real-life experiences add a dose of authenticity to a conversation. Storytelling delights our brains. And the presence of one story seems to evoke a story-sharing response in others, thus continuing conversations.

~~❦~~

Mind maps—visual depictions of the connections of ideas within a larger subject—are regularly used in schoolrooms to teach students how to write. The maps help students to be mindful of what they observe and think.

~~❦~~

3. Think of the conversation as an exploration of a map of your simple-living landscape. Before a conversation, review your mental map of simplicity. Think of all the subjects to which simple living connects and the roadways that join them. Imagine these topics as a map laid out in front of you, a delightful geography of possible conversational destinations. The map can help you maintain a general focus for your conversation, allowing you to wander naturally among subjects while staying within the same general area of thought. Don't forget emotional and spiritual aspects of the landscape; simplicity is not only about macroeconomics, sociology, and environmental stewardship.

4. As you listen and speak, name the place on the simplicity map where you find yourself. Naming subjects or topics in a conversation can be helpful because it helps increase a shared vocabulary. One caution: Too much naming and defining can ruin a conversation by making it into a vocabulary lesson instead of a meandering, enjoyable sharing of thoughts.

5. Focus on conversational prepositions that help you listen deeply to what the other person is saying. Ask yourself what lies under, around, above, inside, behind, or throughout what you are hearing. This mindfulness will draw you toward not only the needs of your conversational partner but also the thought processes.

*Assess the usual list of questions you ask when you meet people.
Which might you change to make your curiosity deeper, your
appreciation more evident, your gratitude more specific?*

6. Listen for emotions, knowledge, and skills. As interesting
    or surprising words and phrases enter your conversation,
    ask yourself what might cause the other person to use
    certain words or phrases. As I have explored Web sites
    of organizations devoted to simple living and engaged
    in conversations with people who have purposely chosen
    to live justly and joyfully, I am struck by their levels of
    education, their high integrity, the panorama of their skills
    and experiences. The same will be true of the people with
    whom you converse.

7. Listen for the strength of verbs and nouns. Strong verbs
    and specific nouns are a good sign; passive verbs and
    generic nouns may indicate passive attitudes or passing
    interest about this subject. An example: I work in a lively
    bureaucracy that does good work among people who are
    poor. But when I am in meetings or reading memos, I look
    carefully for passive verbs that might signal that someone
    is not willing to be proactive, responsible, or transparent.
    This listening and reading helps me understand better
    what the speakers or memo-writers are likely trying to
    accomplish or avoid.

8. Allow and encourage mutual confession and forgiveness.
    Conversations about lifestyle can become intimate very
    quickly. Some of what you hear—or say—will approach the
    qualities of a confession. Don't spoil those moments with
    too-quick reactions or quick diversions away from difficult

subjects. A good way to foster helpful times of confession and forgiveness: Be quiet for a moment or two.

9. Ask good questions. High quality questions engender high quality answers, and conversations grow deeper and broader. What makes a question good? Simply stated, it requires more of the brain's processes to form an answer. So the question, "What do you think about that simplicity book by Bob Sitze?" is better than, "Read any simplicity books lately?" Better yet: "Can you tell me why you read books about simplicity?" You can tell if a question might be engaging large sections of another person's brain when it takes more than a split second for the person to form an answer. In my experience, good questions do the following:

- Invite imaginative answers.
- Are unexpected or unusual.
- Ask for both intellectual and emotional honesty.
- Show appreciation for the person answering the questions.
- Are short, direct, and clear in their intent.

10. Move while you converse. Successful preachers and actors know that movement helps their listeners or audience shift between moods or thoughts. Even the simplest change in position can help bridge the awkward moments when a conversation is heading toward the end of one chapter. In *The Astonishing Hypothesis: The Scientific Search for the Soul*, DNA discoverer Francis Crick notes that attention is invariably drawn to anything that moves. Think how a slight shift in posture, the use of your hands, or even moving a few feet to a different location might increase the strength of your questions or answers.

Stop for a Moment

Go back through what you just read and highlight words or sentences that you want to remember, research further, or try out during your next conversation. Put exclamation points next to or smiley faces around ideas that pleased you. Circle the ideas that suggest your conversational skills could use some polishing. Spill fair-trade coffee, organic green tea, tofu, or yogurt on the places where your jaw dropped open as you were reading.

What Stops a Simple-Living Conversation

While there are ways to enable conversations about simplicity to continue, there are also approaches that can bring these conversations to a halt like a softly slammed door. I know about this because of my now-adult children. In their teenage years, they made it a dinnertime game—usually when we were entertaining visitors—to see who among them could exhibit the greatest skill in torpedoing, maiming, or deflating an otherwise-robust conversation. Their techniques—not printable in a book for church leaders—were masterful. As their father, I came to admire them for their perception about the art of conversation. I also came to understand that their ability to destroy conversations was likely connected to their corresponding ability to engage others in appreciative talk. Fortunately, all three of them have turned out to be caring listeners, brilliant conversationalists, and well-regarded writers, editors, and teachers.

---

*Three Rules of Work: Out of clutter find simplicity; From discord
find harmony; In the middle of difficulty lies opportunity.*
—*Albert Einstein*

Because the conversations they stopped were *mine*, I learned
from my children how easily any verbal exchange can be brought
to an end by the smallest mistake or uncaring behavior. Applying
my children's wisdom to the matter of simple-living conversations,
I offer these few observations about conversation stoppers:

1. Mindful listening requires effort. Concentrating on what
    is being said, both on the surface and under the words
    that you hear, is hard work. If you think that conversation
    is so natural that it doesn't require your whole brain, you
    are *not* likely to engage wholly in the delightful difficulties
    of a working conversation.
2. A simple-living conversation can easily become heavy. The
    rhetoric of simplicity is full of philosophical and spiritual
    principles, axioms of lasting worth, and earnest rhetori-
    cal flourishes that can lose their persuasive power simply
    because of their own weight. Other words that describe
    this conversation-killing condition: overwrought, over-
    the-top, overbearing, or overcomplex.
3. The conversation's emotional thermostat may be set too
    high. Gushings and other emotional outbursts can be
    part of conversations about the most intimate parts of
    people's lives. But when emotional outpourings continue
    ad nauseum, are too intense, or set a tone that can't be
    maintained for long, the conversation necessarily comes to
    a halt—*necessarily* because our brains don't like to sustain
    high emotion.

Misery has enough company. Dare to be happy.
—Volkswagen billboard ad

4. Grim-faced gloom can dissolve a simple-living conversation. From its earliest days until now, the simplicity movement has been branded as a collection of Jeremiahs and social miscreants. (Also communists, those who hate the American way of life, or economic simpletons.) When a simple-living conversation fills with negativity, the tirades and vitriol eventually eat away at the essential goodwill that keeps conversations going. Once again, human brains can't handle the stress of angry, sarcastic, or bitter rhetoric for very long. Without joy, laughter, and imagination, simple-living conversations head downhill quickly.

5. Spiritual truths don't always start or end every conversation. Although simplicity is a spiritual matter, it's not only spiritual. Steering a conversation too quickly toward biblical or doctrinal truths—as though this were the default resting-place for any conversation—might subvert the natural progression of thoughts in that direction. Sometimes the verbiage of religion can destroy concepts and conversations and thus stifle natural language patterns and vocabulary.

6. On the other hand, when simplicity conversations lack spiritual moorings, they might become aimless. Because simple-living conversations are about joyful, abundant living that comes from God's abundance, they are essentially spiritual. This means that a conversation that *never* explores simplicity's spiritual dimensions may also come to a premature ending. The Spirit's presence in these in-

~~~

You, LORD, have saved my life from death, my eyes from tears,
my feet from stumbling.
—Psalm 116:8

~~~

timate exchanges is one of the most powerful experiences you may ever encounter. I can still remember the deeply sacred moments I have experienced in conversations with new friends, participants in my workshops, and colleagues whom I thought I knew well. Because they were spiritually rooted, I have cherished those moments and those people for many years.

7. Speeches eventually lose their audience. A conversation will run its course quickly if one of the participants climbs up on a soapbox or hogs the metaphorical microphone for haranguing, philosophizing, sermonizing, or one-sided storytelling. In my experience, this can easily occur when someone who is living simply—and who has not been listened to by anyone for a long time—suddenly finds an appreciative ear and accepts a little too eagerly the gift of caring listening. How to stop the one-sided pseudo-conversation? Gently interrupt and segue into a connected subject or question.

8. Shallow conversations can easily evaporate. Conversations that stay at the surface of human emotion, intellect, or experience will run out of wind very quickly. People engaged in conversations about their ways of living are often seeking profound meaning and purpose. That's why superficial conversations about simplicity don't continue. One way to avoid shallowness: make matters of simplicity deeply intriguing to all parts of the brain, including propositional truth, emotion, memory, and identity.

The Word of Mouth Marketing Association now claims more than four hundred members. They also claim that they want to keep almost invisible "buzz marketing" ethical. To any of my friends who have volunteered for word-of-mouth marketing: unless I ask you, don't tell me about the products you really like, okay?

9. Discussion may not be enough. The process of discussion proceeds according to implicit rules that engage mostly the forebrain. By contrast, conversation is largely chaotic—its order hard to describe before the conversation begins—and it reaches deeper and wider into the whole brain. How to recognize when the conversation has turned into a mere discussion of ideas? When you stop hearing the pronoun *you* in appreciative questions by either person.

10. Simple-living conversations are generated by a need or by a yearning. People who approach simple living may be coming to the conversation with newly found or newly needed humility. They may have come to the end of their ropes, to the height of their frustrations, or to the bottom of their emotional barrels. If a simplicity conversation tends even subtly toward the supposedly glorious superiority of some specific aspect of simple living, that tone of triumphalism or holier-than-thou condescension can easily put off persons who want to have their humility or their needs understood. The conversation will continue, but it will be empty.

How to "Lead" a Conversation

Eventually you will put down this book and begin conversations about simple living with other people in your congregation. And

～⁓

If you think you are better than others, when you really aren't,
you are wrong. Do your own work well, and then you will have
something to be proud of. But don't compare yourself with others.
We each must carry our own load.
—*Galatians 6:3-5*

～⁓

eventually you will face the daunting prospect of engaging people in warm and welcoming conversations. *Daunting* because lifestyle conversations—like those focused on faith or money—can at first seem stilted or forced.

Let's spend some time thinking together how you might be both participant and leader in a conversation about simplicity.

1. Think of yourself as participant first, as leader second. This doubled mindfulness is familiar territory, because your brain already knows how to assign priorities to several different—even competing—roles or functions. Although you cannot multitask—be both leader and participant at the same moment—you can flip back and forth rapidly between those roles, momentarily holding one or the other as the highest priority or the most pleasurable.

    As you engage in a simple-living conversation, you participate fully in the give-and-take of the conversation. But the leader part of you is also holding at ready a set of goals, some conversational directions, the simplicity map I noted earlier. Because you are trying to be a good listener, your ears are keyed to attend to certain words and phrases. Some of that language will be important to you as participant, other words and phrases significant to you as the conversation's facilitator.

2. You don't have to spark, direct, or initiate the conversation. You can lead by following. This means that you don't ask

Right now, look at your hands as the source for a prayer. Thank God for what your hands can do, who or what they'll touch today, and the blessings you extend through your hands. If you like, fold them while you pray . . .

every question (that's an interview) or answer every question (that's an outdated teacher/student model). Leading from behind may mean that you wait for promising moments to ask good questions or offer your thoughts. This form of leadership also encourages you to be a facilitator, drawing out otherwise-quiet participants to offer their insights or questions.

3. Lead with questions. I have spoken about good questions earlier, and when you find the right moment to ask those questions, they can be even more effective. The right moment? It might be when:

- a previously quiet person shows interest in speaking.
- an intriguing possibility—idea, emotion, story-starter—invites further exploration.
- further clarity—definitions, examples, supporting logic—would cement an idea or a discovery in place.
- you sense that a conversant wants to say more but is hesitant about talking too much.
- it's time to shift the focus to another connected subject or person.
- you disagree with something that has been said.

4. Keep in mind your conceptual map of simplicity. If you have made this mental diagram, you can put it to good use

~~~

I find it interesting that the meanest life, the poorest existence, is attributed to God's will, but as human beings become more affluent, as their living standard and style begin to ascend the material scale, God descends the scale of responsibility at a commensurate speed.
—Maya Angelou

~~~

as a leader in a conversation. Especially if you will continue the conversation over several occasions, the map will help you remember the content of previous conversations and prepare for subsequent gatherings.

5. Be satisfied if you fulfill your goals only partially. Remember that conversations only *start* a process of social change. This means that even the most exquisite sharing will not necessarily fulfill your hopes for long-term change in your congregation. Learn to accept these starting places as worthwhile beginnings for the journeys of lifestyle change that will take place over the coming years.

6. Choose carefully the place and the occasion for the conversation. If you are the person who initiates these conversations, think of the best venues available to you. (For Pat in the previous chapter, a local breakfast diner was an especially helpful atmosphere.) Because you want mutual exchanges to take place easily, consider the level of noise or distraction in those places. Will you be sheltered from the sometimes-quickened pace of commerce? How bright and cheery will the surroundings be? Will you be able to remain in that place undisturbed for a longer period? Will the conversation take place at a time that allows for measured thought? Will you offer food and beverages to

Someone told me recently that my ideas were hard to keep up with. It got me to thinking, "Is simple living hard to keep up with or hard to slow down to?" I'm still wondering about the question.

help keep energy levels high? (For other thoughts, see the section "Finding Good Places and Situations for Conversations" on pages 156–9)

7. Continue to be forthright about this subject. Maintain your sense of personal mission, your sharp critique of contemporary culture, and your resolve to keep simple living important for the people you love and serve. As a respectful participant in a conversation about simple living, you can still be a persuasive leader.

8. Show appreciation for those engaged in the conversation. "Appreciative inquiry" is now a respected method for fundraising and a highly efficient means of planning. Mutual appreciation is also the foundation upon which a lifestyle conversation can be built. You will be seen as an effective leader if you continually show admiration for other people's attempts at lifestyle change, especially if you value those who are struggling just to find the right questions. Remember that your leadership is most effective when you build up the confidence and skill of others.

9. Have fun staying on track while straying. I work among highly passionate and highly skilled church professionals. I learned from them long ago that no one controls a conversation. I have also discovered that during supposedly out-of-control conversations—even silly ones—some of the best thinking takes place; the most innovative possibilities suddenly take shape and the most fervent friendships

come to life. Although as its leader you will be attempting to keep the conversation on track—somewhere in the simplicity ballpark—you can also think of yourself as someone who is riding the currents in an ocean of conversational possibilities. Even people who stray from the supposed subject are, in their own mind, adding to the weight of an argument, the cogency of a story, the worth of a comment. Have fun with this wonderful tension. If you don't, your nervous attempts to rein in the conversation may in fact make it even less focused.

10. Stay calm. This is the hardest leadership quality for me to exhibit. I have had to learn to be quieter, slower, and more patient. Fortunately, I have benefited from the example and tutelage of some noted simple-living pioneers who are humble and whose brains don't run on caffeine and adrenaline like mine.

Especially during their first moments, conversations about simplicity can become an excited celebration of mutual interests. That is one way of describing what happens when people hitherto unknown to each other suddenly discover all the things they have in common. In those cases—and throughout all simplicity conversations—you can maintain the flow of ideas and the quality of the sharing by remaining engagingly calm. Perhaps you could serve milk and cookies instead of coffee?

Stop for a Moment

Take some time to think about what I might have left out of our imagined mealtime conversation. What fact or idea do you still need to know before you start your own conversations? What imagined difficulty am I overlooking? What part of your passion or determination did I not acknowledge? Write your thoughts in the margins of the previous few pages. And get ready for the dessert menu . . .

~~✺~~

Finding Good Places and Situations for Conversations

Philosopher, consultant, management guru, and author Peter Block offers this simple advice to aspiring consultants: choose carefully the room in which you will meet. Block understands that mental acuity and focused attention require physical comfort. Fresh air, adequate lighting, comfortable seating, ample space for movement, quiet, an engaging view—these all contribute to the quality of a conversation. In the matter of simple living, I would add in something about making sure the setting exemplifies simplicity.

Let's use a few moments now to think together about the places and situations in which your simple-living conversations might take place. I will list those that have worked for me as well as those that I can imagine would be workable. You can think alongside me, perhaps writing your own ideas in the margins here.

Places and situations in which simple-living conversations might take place include the following:

Breakfast: The day is young, the world a little more quiet, and you have the opportunity to be with people when most of them are at the height of their biorhythmic capabilities.

Lunch: The experiences of the morning lie fresh on people's memories, and their need to interpret their lives is met by this midday break. A refreshing conversation in the middle of a day's goings and comings.

Shared dessert: These end-of-day moments can be like grace notes or the cadenza at the end of a violin concerto. For church

~~≈~~

The next time you take a walk, see how slowly you can meander toward a destination. Stop along the way to examine small things and small events. Think of each one as the start of a significant story.

~~≈~~

folks, a time of conversation about simple living might be a welcome substitute for evening meetings at church. Because it delights palates and eyes, the food you eat will be a good symbol for the conversation.

Walk-and-talk experiences. The thrill of a meaningful conversation combines with the brain-invigorating benefits of exercise. Strollers benefit from the exercising of their bodies and their brains. The destination for the walk may also be part of the enjoyment.

Parks, patios, and outside venues. At the side of a pond, on a park bench, sitting in the afternoon sun, perched on a boulder, or sitting on the lawn—all are evocative scenes for honest and open conversation about what is truly important.

Community or neighborhood events. Wherever people gather, they talk. Soccer matches, school events, festivals and parades, community forums, cultural events, charity walks, summer concerts in the park—these are familiar examples of times when neighbors join with each other in enjoyable experiences. Depth is not always a requirement for these conversations, but honesty and being helpful are.

Book-reading groups. Because discussing the book usually leads to a plethora of other subjects and sharings, these gatherings bring with them the implicit promise of meaningful conversation. This particular topic may bind a group together in new ways.

Congregational small group ministry. The setting of these groups encourages a natural vocabulary and emotionally honest sharing. Just one conversation about lifestyle could start a longer series of conversations or study of simple living.

I spend time on Saturday mornings at the park-district center, taking tai chi classes. The reason: this martial art is best practiced slowly, quietly, and with great appreciation for the smallest details of hand placement, posture, and balance. Tai chi has become a symbol for serenity in my life. I'm also learning to defend myself against extremely slow attackers.

Devotional moments before meetings: Personal, prayerful conversations about what's important—these can offer a wonderful start to any meeting. Scriptural connections add to participants' witness.

Conversations to end a sermon: At the end of the proclamation of God's word comes a simple invitation: "Turn to one or two nearby persons; talk about how what you have just heard will help you make sense of the week to come." In a few moments, the sermon wiggles its way into worshipers' working memory, gaining relevance and utility during these short exchanges.

An overnight retreat: The magic of the night's darkness adds emphasis to the prospect that conversations will last longer and delve deeper into participants' innermost yearnings.

A road trip: When you travel, you can talk. The atmosphere inside a car, bus, or motor home encourages honest sharing. The longer the trip, the more the conversation can cover.

Homes: In the comfort and familiarity of their own setting, people are more honest about who they are and what's important to them. Surrounded by the artifacts of their lifestyle choices, they also can talk about their specific hopes or triumphs.

Caught moments in the normal life of a congregation: These short encounters might be the first place for you to focus efforts. Caught moments include parking lot conversations before or after worship services or meetings; table talk at congregational meals or coffee hours; friendly banter during times of fellowship and formal or informal welcomings.

> *Too many people spend money they haven't earned,*
> *to buy things they don't want, to impress people they don't like.*
> *—Attributed to Will Rogers*

Phone calls: The utilitarian checking-in phone call is also an underrated-yet-powerful mode of caring. These unannounced packets of thoughtfulness can become a time of mutual gratitude and appreciation.

Letter writing: Whether boosted by electronic means or blessed merely by an envelope and a stamp, written conversations can foster lasting relationships. The pen pals of the distant past have now become cell-phone, MySpace, and Instant-Messaging friends. The effect is the same: Eventually people talk to each other about what's important. Even teens.

Counseling at times of crisis: Because many life crises—divorces, economic hardship, parent-child relationships, health issues—are connected to lifestyle considerations, the precepts of simple living may become part of hopeful counseling.

Repurposed caring ministry leaders: Former participants in now-dormant caring programs—for example, Stephen Ministry—most likely still retain their capacities for lifestyle-related conversations. Without trying to restart the programs, you might encourage these trained caregivers to engage in simple-living conversations on an informal basis.

Staying Emotionally and Intellectually Honest

You have read about honesty several times in this book. I stress this part of simple living because emotional and intellectual honesty—with yourself and with others—is one of the greatest gifts that can come from conversations about lifestyle. I want to emphasize that

<hr />

We should help people whenever we can, especially if they are followers of the Lord.
—Galatians 6:10

<hr />

fact here again and encourage you to maintain your integrity as you engage in conversations about this subject.

Not that you are dishonest, dear lunchtime friend. But like all of us who are trying to live joyfully and justly on the Earth, you face multiple temptations to speak in euphemisms, to hide your deepest emotions, or to disregard the emotions of others. You may face angry responses when you ask hard, perhaps impolite questions about the ways in which this society is fouling its own nest. You may wallow in false humility because you are still on the simplicity journey, not an expert or a perfect example. You may face guilt, embarrassment, or shame as you choose to live differently than others. And you may wrestle with a judgmental spirit, a feeling of loneliness, or other emotions that are not helpful. Each of these facets of leadership can tempt you to soften or dumb down your message, overlook what's wrong in the world, mask your emotions, or even drop out of your relationships with people who don't understand what you are trying to do or say.

Both intellectual and emotional honesty are also a necessary part of your personal equipment as one who wants to help others along the way. The economic, environmental, spiritual, and relational messes on this planet are not going to disappear if we are afraid to speak the truth in love. Some examples: Obesity is not going away if we overlook our ability to help those closest to us reduce this problem before it reduces them to ill health. Carbon loading the atmosphere is not going to diminish if we let non-scientists prevail in the argument about the nature of global warm-

~~✦~~

As a preteen, I valued people who were "hairy." These were men and women whose feet were on the ground, who spoke their minds plainly, who didn't put on airs, and who got things done. Mostly they were my teachers, which is probably why I became one. As for having actual hair, I have failed them baldly (sic).

~~✦~~

ing or pollution. The state of this country's economy is not going to heal itself by revving up the engines of greed and consumption while we stand by quietly. As you show integrity in every conversation you engage in, you can overcome the temptation to shade the truth, ignore facts, or hide your feelings.

Emotional and intellectual honesty is also a gift of God for the world God loves. People who have been hiding their presumed middle-class lifestyle behind mounting credit-card debt can benefit from a gracious, kind, and insistent conversation about the short-lived happiness that comes from purchasing things they really don't need. Colleagues who can't seem to decide what they want to do with their lives might derive relief from hearing someone question their perpetual wandering among purposes. Folks who scurry through their lives at the speed of stress can be helped enormously by an insistent friend's emotional pleading to slow down or shed their need for constant motion. People who are addicted to substances or stuff can be relieved when someone else honestly names their self-destructive behavior for what it really is. Overweight or obese friends can be helped, when asking their most difficult question, by the difficult-but-honest answer: "Yes, you look fat in that dress, in those pants, with that makeup, with those accessories, in that car, in that restaurant, and with those new toys."

Your honesty can be both necessary and beneficial. Don't get tempted to disregard the worth of your integrity.

～✦～

According to the findings of the World Health Organization,
as of September 2006 the world has more overweight people
(one billion) than undernourished people (about six hundred
million). Experts now warn of an obesity pandemic. They're
not exaggerating.

～✦～

Finding Help Nearby

You may find it difficult to start or to continue simplicity conversations. Sooner or later you may come up against the limits of your own skills or get tired of trying so hard to help people simplify their lives. At some point in this conversation-starting process, you may just want to have a conversation that isn't purposed, that doesn't require sharp listening, that lets you relax in the presence of other people. That's when you may need to find help to keep working at simplicity.

Asking for that help may be hard for you, even when you need and want it. I know how that happens because I come from a long line of people who would rather help than be helped. Proud peasants on one branch of my family tree and eccentric gentry on the other—neither of them particularly skilled in the arts of humility, seeking help, or receiving assistance. My kinfolks would rather go hungry than ask for food, shiver than ask for a coat, invent home remedies than go to a doctor, and muddle through a relationship problem than get assistance from a professional counselor. We are sturdy folks, we Sitzes, and also just a little thickheaded when it comes to asking someone to lend a hand.

As you find other people with whom to talk about simple living, don't be like me or my progenitors. Ask for help when you need it. These observations might be helpful:

This week add 30 minutes to your nightly sleep, next week another 30 minutes. Each week keep adding minutes until you wake up most mornings totally refreshed. Now adjust your schedule expectations so you get that much sleep every night.

1. Remember that many people—invisible to you if you don't ask them about themselves—are struggling with their own lifestyles and would love to talk with you. I have showed you how to find them.
2. Unless your whole spirit is unraveling like knitting attacked by a kitten, tackle the smallest details first. Sometimes a good night's sleep or one "I'm sorry" can broaden your outlook and firm your resolve.
3. Talk with your pastor. Most likely he or she shares the same life experiences as you when it comes to simple living. Most likely your pastor would welcome the chance to think through your mutual lifestyle questions with you.
4. Don't think of *help* as "solving problems." Instead, ask for assistance as a way of increasing your capabilities, achieving realistic goals, gaining perspective, doing God's will.
5. And if your whole spirit is coming apart, think about leaving these simplicity conversations alone for a while. Sometimes letting ground lie fallow improves its ability to nurture crops. A sabbath might be just what you need to restore your soul, resort your priorities, rethink your strategies and review your blessings—without the weight of the world on your shoulders.

One more observation—and encouragement—from my personal experience. Here and in other places I write about purpose-

To all who knew me as a congregational leader in my earlier years: Forgive me for burning you up, wearing you down, tiring you out. Back then I thought that we would succeed if we worked hard, planned well, and executed our plans with excellence. Now I know what I did to you. Sorry.

greed, my way of describing what is sometimes called "a messiah complex." The people who know me well would name this as one of *my* faults. I live continuously with the feeling that not much time is left for me to get done all that I have been called to do in life. Some think of me as impatient, aggressive, or even uncaring as I push at goals; insist on excellence; and coax, drive, and pull others along with me. Sometimes what I need most from those who can help me is their insistent reminder that I am not in charge of simplicity, not in control of anything except myself, not able to change anyone else. That I'm not God and that the One who is almighty and loving Savior is already satisfied with my stewardship of life.

Does any of this help?

Finding Courage

We are coming to the end of this lunchtime conversation, so let me finish with one more reflection, this one about courage. As I survey the landscape of simplicity—its philosophy, its theology, its habits and practices—I am convinced that the key to changing my lifestyle and yours is to act with courageous integrity. To do what we say we believe, even at some risk to ourselves.

To be personal again, this admission: I already know enough about the connection of simplicity to global warming, the destruction of species, the injustice of hunger and poverty, the plagues

~~≈~~

*As [you simplify your] life, the laws of the universe will appear
less complex, and solitude will not be solitude, nor poverty poverty, nor weakness weakness.*
—Henry David Thoreau

~~≈~~

of greed and disregard that gobble up relationships. I have read
enough lists of 101 Things You Can Do to keep me busy 101 hours
a day. I read E. F. Schumacher's classic *Small Is Beautiful* when it
was first published, and I have been reading the Bible since I was
six years old. I have filled my personal journals with musings about
these matters. But none of this is important unless I continue to
make the small, incremental changes that lead toward simplicity,
manageability, and sustainability: Buying differently, saving more
carefully, observing and appreciating more thankfully, loving others
more dearly, consuming less wastefully, giving away more cheer-
fully, and finding joy more deeply.

To take my own simplicity conversations beyond shared hypocrisy, I must find the courage to match my righteous attitudes
about simplicity and thorough knowledge of its precepts and
practices with specific decisions that honor the spirit and the letter
of simplicity. You understand what I'm saying, right?

"How to find courage?" you ask. The following ideas may
seem simple, but they work for me:

- Stay connected to Jesus and to the church he established.
  Fill your mind with Christ's example and teachings. Pillow
  yourself in the cloud of witnesses who are the people of
  God. Center yourself in the Scriptures to gain perspective
  about the history of God's will for the world.
- Enter all simplicity conversations with the prayer that God
  will strengthen you through the example of other courageous people.

- Look and listen carefully to the people around you. Think of every encounter with other faithful people of God as a free education in simple living—either as example or as warning.
- Look and listen for the small places in life where courage is evident: newspaper stories, the wisdom and witness of people who are poor, chance conversations with strangers, children who ask why, and followers who challenge their leaders.
- Trust forgiveness. It can cure you of your blindness and deafness to God's voice.
- Review or assay the ways in which you are already courageous. In your journals, e-mails, remembered conversations, and personal history you may see a person already possessing high integrity, already able to act courageously. Perhaps you can find courage in yourself?

Stop for a Moment

That was a nice lunch; thanks for sharing your time with me. I have enjoyed the conversation and learned a lot. I look forward to another time with you soon. Can I ask a favor before you turn the page, an odd one? Could you put down this book for one week—or if you are really excited about what you have read, for one day—and let everything you have read soak into your brain a little deeper? While you are away, I'm going to be getting ready to help you make some plans about what you will do when you finish this book. For now, close the book and spend some time away from our conversation. See you soon.

6

After You've Gone

W hen I know a pleasing conversation is about to end, I feel sad that the experience will soon be over. Another challenge presents itself: how to end the conversation in a memorable way. Usually my conversation partners and I add one or two last words, hoping that they will be the ones most remembered. Ideally, when the moment of goodbye finally takes place, those final thoughts become a good motivator for us to put into practice what we have talked about.

That's what I hope this chapter will do for our conversation—you and me, the rumpled guy in jeans you first met so many pages ago. I want to offer you a few insights that I hope you will remember after we have parted, ideas that will motivate you to implement the decisions you have tentatively made about simplicity conversations in your congregation.

Leaving a Legacy

In conversations we leave our mark on other people. The words of other people imprint their emotions and personalities on us, too. The contents of our conversations stick to our souls like the taste of a first kiss, and we become our conversations just like we become what we eat. We remember best the parts of the conversation that affect our emotions, our will, our sense of identity, or our

~~❦~~

*Recently I went to the wedding of a colleague where the pastor
said about the couple, "They see their life together as a way by
which the world will change." How gratifying to see two people
mature enough to transform one of society's most materialistic
moments into a time of witness and encouragement. I should
have lunch with them sometime.*

~~❦~~

purpose in life. Just as each of us leaves a legacy at our death, we
also leave behind something valuable in each personal conversation
in which we engage.

As you take part in conversations about simplicity, you are
leaving something valuable and truthful behind, some ideas or
personal traits that can be remembered and acted upon. Together
with others, you have activated imagination, imparted courage,
appreciated what is important to the other person(s), and modeled
emotional and intellectual honesty. People will remember what
occurs during these conversations, and they will carry the shared
words in their minds like precious cargo.

Legacies are especially poignant for me as I write, because
just a few months ago I participated in the memorial service for
my father, who died peacefully in his sleep at the grandly blessed
age of 91. Because he did not like to draw attention to himself,
my father probably had no idea about his legacy. He certainly understood that his children and grandchildren loved him, that they
believed as he believed and lived as he lived. But he would not have
imagined that his legacy—what he gave to others in conversation
and in actions—would affect so many others with whom he came
in contact. His humility kept him from seeing the wider worth of
his life.

I hope you are aware of the impact of your words. Think about
how deeply and broadly your shared thoughts—and the thoughts

Every Sunday for two months, include in the prayers at worship
a petition about contentment. See if this repeated prayer draws
comments or questions, one way or the other.

others will share with you—can spread into other places, other situations, other groups. As you start and continue conversations about simple living, you are passing on a valuable legacy. Don't be too humble about this very good thing you are doing.

Starting Something Good (Again)

While reading this book—including the thoughts in the margins—you have heard my implied invitation to remember how you got started on this simple-living journey. Somewhere in your dusty or polished past was a moment or a person that influenced you—or tipped you—to reverse your opinions about usual societal norms and to seek simplicity instead. In turn, that good start engendered just enough emotion to motivate you to other actions, like reading this book.

Simplicity conversations might be for you a restart. But for someone else these conversations might be their first experience in questioning the way their lives are progressing, *their* first encounter with someone who practices simplicity, *their* first opportunity to tell someone else about their deepest hopes and darkest fears about their lifestyles, or *their* first friendship with someone who thinks like they do.

Think of each of these conversations, then, as a gift you give to others who want to start toward a new way of thinking and living but have never been given the permission to run, walk, hop, or skip toward a goal different from Western culture's usual "more

When our children were very young, Chris and I would answer their questions about our family's decidedly different ways of living with the Ultimate Parental Nondiscussable Notice: "Because that's (not) who we are." In other words, our strong identity compelled our strong lifestyle actions or nonactions.

and better." Just as good questions encourage good answers, your good-start conversations will encourage good-life journeys.

Experiencing Integrity

Simple living requires a healthy dose of integrity—which means that you do what you say you believe. Given the general direction of Western society, when you choose simplicity over its opposite philosophies, you are carving out a difficult path over some very high mountains. What will carry you and others on a simplicity journey may be a stubbornness about doing what's right. Perhaps this is another way to describe integrity.

In your conversations with others about the practice of simple living, you are going to notice varying levels of integrity. Some of your conversational partners may strongly uphold their values by their actions, while others may have strong feelings or great hopes for simplicity they are not able to put into practice.

In his various writings about effective living, self-help sage Stephen Covey talks about how to reclaim integrity. "Make one promise to yourself," he says, "and keep it!" Then make and keep another promise to yourself, and keep doing this. Eventually you will find yourself in the habit of being true to your values. Remember that each time you and others speak with integrity, the conversations will be a gracious gift of God's Spirit.

~⋙⋘~

Greed-lock—a paralysis of movement toward life goals while you accumulate enough stuff to help you get there.

~⋙⋘~

Confronting Your Own Hypocrisy

At the same time you work on your integrity, you will have to face its opposite, hypocrisy. Even the most ardent simple-living adherents learn to deal with their own duplicity. Because their sensibilities are more finely tuned than others, they hold themselves to more stringent requirements about simple living. And so they have also learned to forgive themselves for their double standards. They finally come to the point where they live with the small disconnect between what they believe and what they do.

As you participate in conversations about simplicity, you will eventually reckon with your own self-deceptions about your lifestyle, naming sins and shortcomings while at the same time asking for forgiveness. Think of your conversations not only as a way to purge yourself of the small lies that might still plague your journey toward simplicity, but also as a way by which God's Spirit names the selfish part of you and keeps it from ever gaining complete control.

Living in Tension

The conversations in which you take part may increase the tension you feel between wanting to change Western culture and dropping out partially or completely. You may not decide to learn Spanish fluently and live in a Central American village for the rest of your life, writing poetry about people who are poor and oppressed. But by their honesty and depth your conversations might pull you in a similar direction.

───❦───

There are two things, Lord, I want you to do for me before I die:
Make me absolutely honest and don't let me be too poor or too
rich. Give me just what I need.
—Proverbs 30:7-8

───❦───

I understand that pressure. When we first became parents, Chris and I dropped out of our privileged leadership positions in our congregations and went to live in an intentional Christian community in the forests of northern California. We wanted our daily lives to be consonant with our beliefs about the nature of the Christian life. Our need for harmony between our values and behaviors compelled us to try to find an alternative way to live among a different kind of people.

With the other members of that faith community, we soon found that the new setting and new friends only partially redeemed us from our previous lifestyles. We lived among trees and tree lovers, of course, but we still had to reckon with new temptations to acquisitiveness or life-wasting pleasures, new ways to forget about our health and wholeness, and new kinds of hurried living and wrongheaded worrying. The difficulties remained essentially the same, only now they had trees attached to them.

Eventually we came back into the mainstream of society, strengthened by those years of living in majestic mountain splendor to face the challenges of living in conventional culture again. One strong lesson: wherever we lived, we would always choose *not* to participate in selected parts of the world around us—to drop out in small ways and thus not to honor or support what is unhealthy, unproductive, ungodly in the culture around us. We also learned that the forest offered only tree-deep simplicity, not any more conducive to godly living than the strawberry patch in your garden or the view from the second-hand chairs on your front porch.

In your conversations about simple living, you may find your-selves heightening your disdain for contemporary culture or the setting in which you are living now. Whether or not you decide to resolve the tension by moving away from worldly influences, think of the conversations as a source for perspective, forgiveness, and joy.

~≈≈~

Stop for a Moment

Take a moment to consider the times in your simplicity journey when hypocrisy has dismantled your integrity or where your integrity has diminished possible hypocrisy. Give each of these situations a name—for example, The Keep the Children Happy Puzzle or The Brand Names Knot—so that you can share your integrity/hypocrisy tensions in each case. And if you have dropped out—or are considering it—give that experience a name, too, and be ready to talk about that experience.

~≈≈~

Howling at the Moon

In *Not Trying Too Hard: New Basics for Sustainable Congregations* (Alban Institute, 2001), I had some fun with the image of leaders who were just a little too aware of their righteousness, excoriating supposedly evil persons, and consigning imagined other sinners to hellish punishment. What I was trying to emphasize is this: point-ing out evil may be a necessary evil, but it's not the foundation for a sustainable congregation. Pointing out others' malfeasance is not the basis for simplicity conversations, either.

I know a woman who, over the years, partially furnished her home and clothed herself and her son with items that had been discarded in the trash cans in the alley behind her home. She also keeps track of every one of her moderate expenses and every penny of income. The people who know her well think of her as abundantly joyful and generous. They're probably right.

As you necessarily identify what is *not* good or helpful about contemporary life, think, too, about what gives you joy, what's useful, what helps you with your life purpose, what enhances healthy relationships, what keeps you going on tough days. The most seasoned veterans of simple living that I know have found ways to celebrate life fully, not siphoning off their joy into pickle-barrel stinginess or disdain of other people. They appreciate not only the grandeur of a sunset on a cool summer evening but also the sound of cool jazz at a public concert in the park. They not only relish the taste of a simple bacon, lettuce, and tomato sandwich, but can also appreciate the delicate flavors of a glass of fine wine. They understand partying, dancing, laughing, exercising, and feeling good.

Howling will get you some attention—and motivate others to bay and bark, too—but it's not going to do much more than to increase your anger, flood your brain with stress chemicals, and diminish your usefulness in changing the world.

Think of your simple-living conversations as a way to sidestep the frustration of yowling and yammering at evil. Think of the people with whom you converse as God-given evidence of the abundant blessings that peek out of every corner of your life. Use the conversations to increase your hope and pleasure in being a positive force for God's will in the world.

Do not wait for leaders; do it alone, person to person.
—*Mother Teresa*

Insisting that George Do Something

One of the warnings I paste on the inside of my brain goes something like this: don't ask others to do for you something you can darn well do for yourself. I neither live with a sense of entitlement nor live in a world where others serve my every wish. But I am still tempted to act like a manipulative trickster who sloughs off responsibility by getting others to do his work.

I think my interior self-help poster might apply to your simplicity conversations, too. Here's how: If in your conversations you talk mostly about what others might do—or not do—to improve the world, you might be falling into a trap of self-deception that ignores or diminishes your personal responsibility or capability for change. While it's good that consumers challenge corporations, while it's certainly true that legislation might help curb our wastrel society, and while we can hope for others to hold us accountable, these activities can also become ways for us to avoid taking specific, individual actions to change our own lives close at hand, among people close to us.

Think of your simplicity conversations as a way to gain courage and insight first for your own changed lifestyle and you will avoid the self-deception that Jesus mocks in his words about splinters and logs in people's eyes.

Engaging Children and Youth

Your conversations about simplicity may involve children and teenagers who pay attention to you. Given the amount of self-

A few weeks ago, I noticed a dad and mom shopping in the grocery store. They were also using the occasion to help their little kids understand the meaning of "No, we don't need that." I congratulated the parents and thanked them, too.

determination and money that many young people are afforded in our society, you may want to consider them a first-choice audience for your simplicity conversations. Teens and children are already the targets for massive marketing campaigns that not only sell them the stuff of supposedly good lives but also determine what constitutes quality living.

Unless you are already very good with kids—including your own—you may easily fall into the role of the wiser adult telling the children what to do. Not a bad role, of course, but probably not well suited to the conversational ethic I'm proposing here. Also not an especially effective role to take if you truly desire a long-lasting relationship that will become the seedbed for long-lasting change.

As strange as this sounds, you might become a credible witness for children and teens when you don't try to be a credible witness. Because they are already exposed to persuasive speech—television, technology, and their friends—at every turn, children and teens may not be as receptive of your persuasive utterances as you would hope. That's when true conversation wins out.

The conversations that I'm advocating in this book may be persuasive simply because they don't try to persuade. Good and respectful questions, true dialogue, appreciative solicitation of stories, the absence of knee-jerk condemnation of youth culture—these all contribute to deepened relationships that eventually influence children and teens.

~~✦~~

Invent several aphorisms—short, whimsical proverbs—about simplicity and write them onto cards or construction paper. Place these miniposters in places where they will remind you of the wisdom you have learned from others and of your resolve to live simply.

~~✦~~

How to find and invite children and teens into earnest conversation about their present and future lives? I have the inkling that children and teens respond to the same stimuli and invitations as do adults. In other words, most of what you have read in this book probably works with children and youth.

Having said that, I'm aware that in many congregations, children and youth are segregated from the general congregational population for supposed special treatment. In those places, young members rarely have the chance to be part of cross-generational experiences, to be included in the rich mix of congregational demography, to learn from and teach people who are older or younger than themselves. Adding insult to injury, your congregation may operate with the notion that only professionally trained church workers have the skills—and congregational blessing—to engage children and youth in their faith development.

How might you include children and youth in mixed-age conversational groups? Here are some of my thoughts:

1. When you invite adults into the conversations, ask them to invite any of their children or teenagers—and their friends—to the conversation.
2. Choose venues—for example, someone's home—where children or youth might already be present.

The number of one-hundred-year-olds in the United States tallied in the census of 2000: 50,740. The number estimated for 2050: 1,149,500.
—*U.S. Census Bureau, reported in "Harper's Index,"* Harper's Magazine, *February 2006*

3. Place the conversation into an activity in which all ages can participate. For example, the walk-and-talk format for conversations could be a hike, a fund-raising event, a bike ride, or a family retreat.

4. Use traditional congregational activities aimed at youth as occasions to introduce the ideals of simple living. For example, a youth forum, a Sunday morning gathering, or a session of confirmation class might serve as a starting point for later conversations.

5. With parental permission and guidance, invite some teenagers to begin and maintain a blog or MySpace conversation about this subject. You can serve as coach, editor, or mentor in the process, again with parental permission and partnership.

6. If you are a pastor, don't overlook the possibility of including the wisdom of simple living in your sermons and children's messages. In those cases, always encourage children and teens to continue with their parents the conversation you have begun with your teaching.

As you include children and teens in these simplicity conversations, you will provide them with a view of the good life that counteracts the materialistic, consumptive lifestyle messages that might otherwise overwhelm them.

Stop for a Moment

Many congregations—yours, perhaps?—live with the desperate self-judgment that sounds something like this: "We don't have any young people in the congregation anymore." My appraisal of simple living is that it's a hot topic among young adults—and some teens. It might be possible that your congregation could become attractive to these age groupings simply because you are talking about something important to them. How might that work in your setting?

Showing Your Earnest Side

Over the years of my adult life I have come to see the power of "earnest." I have been attracted to the piercing glance of total strangers, brought up short by the loving gaze of my spouse, and found personal solidarity with people in other countries within moments of first meeting them. All because I could see the intensity in their faces. As a student and observer of neurobiology for about 30 years now, I understand how earnest expression can be persuasive: all of us immediately recognize in the faces of certain people that they truly believe what they are saying or doing, and we feel compelled to believe what they believe and to do what they are doing. Although skilled pathological liars can also easily convince us by their brand of sincerity, we can, for the most part, separate truth from lies and will usually follow the lead of someone whose deep conviction is apparent in their facial expressions—mostly in their eyes and mouth.

Love is a fruit in season at all times and within the reach of every hand.
—*Mother Teresa*

You can read faces and other people can read yours. The look in your eye can be as persuasive as the most well-reasoned, well-researched, and well-spoken discourse. I tell you this so that you understand that your own genuineness will show in your face. In other words, trust the power of your earnest look when you talk about these matters. Even if you *are* shy.

Deciding about Programs

It may seem inevitable in your situation: conversation participants get excited about what they are discovering together and decide to move the benefits farther into the lifeblood of the congregation. This natural evolution of programs may occur as a matter of course in your congregation; you might get ready for that possibility without encouraging it. These thoughts come to mind:

1. Think how simple living could be part of the work of an already existing congregational group, event, or function. For example, your stewardship team may want to integrate simplicity into an annual funding program or a hunger awareness group may see the connections of simple living to their goals.

2. If the conversation group wants to take action on a specific project, decide carefully how much time it will take, the resources it will require, and the means by which you will know when you have fulfilled your objectives. In this way

Using a Bible lexicon or word-finding tool, list all the scripture references you can find that extol prosperity, material wealth, pleasure, happiness, or other supposed qualities of "the good life." Do the same with concepts like generosity, sharing, sacrifice, sufficiency, or contentment. Contrast the two lists.

you won't be tempted to form yet another church committee, task force, or team.

3. As the group moves from conversation to congregationally oriented action, give members the option of *not* engaging in the program, and continue your schedule of informal conversations. You may also want to begin simplicity conversations with an entirely new group of friends.

4. Consider some actions that move beyond conversation but stop short of creating another congregational function:

- Explore individually the Web sites of other simple-living organizations and share what you have discovered. (See "Resources" at the end of this book for current examples.)
- Visit the simplicity circles or conversation groups at another congregation, seeing what they have learned and sharing what you know.
- Set aside a portion of every conversation for sharing about news articles, features in journals, personal correspondence, or other assigned readings or tasks.
- Focus on specific topics or questions for a while, taking advantage of some personal research while not forsaking the general conversational tone of the group's time together.

*You know that our Lord Jesus Christ was kind enough to give up
all his riches and become poor, so that you could become rich.*
—2 Corinthians 8:9

- Set up a pen pal arrangement with other simplicity folks, perhaps a similar group in another congregation, the leader of a simple-living organization, a treasured friend in another country, or a simplicity blogger. (See "Resources" for ideas on this subject.)
- Spend time during each conversation to talk about your reactions and thoughts regarding a specific situation, problem, or possibility faced by one of the group's members. Keep the discussion personal.
- Secure an editorial column or space in your congregational newsletter or local newspaper using the insights of this group as thought-provoking material to be shared with a wider group.

5. Stay flexible in this matter, being open to the possibilities that present themselves as the conversations grow more and more valuable for more and more people.

Ending the Conversations

They never *really* end, of course. Once begun, your simplicity conversations will continue, if only in the memories of each participant. As an informal group that gets together from time to time, though, you and your simplicity friends may decide to bring the conversations to an end for a while. This is wise, helpful, and perhaps necessary. You probably already know how to end a conversation, and you may already have a sense when a group has come to the end of its usefulness. Here are some of my observations, under the general title, "How to Know When You're Done Talking":

1. You find the same subjects getting picked apart without anything new being said.
2. You realize that it's turned into a gripe session, an opportunity to roast the pastor or some other leader, or an emotion dump.
3. You notice that it's virtually impossible, given your busy schedules, for you to find time to talk with each other.
4. You see that personality conflicts, significant disagreements, or inability to converse naturally are occurring too frequently.
5. You notice that participants no longer seem interested, honest, or stimulated.
6. The group gets too big for personal dialogue or devolves into mere discussion of the subject. (Then you can split the group into several smaller groups.)

Goodbye, Then

It's time to say goodbye. I wish God's blessing on your conversations and on whatever occurs among the people with whom you converse. I would love to be there among you, to learn from you about what's important, and to get excited about the things you share.

Excitement is an important by-product of these conversations, because this emotion can carry you and others into the rest of your life, where you will meet and energize other rumpled-shirt people, other kindred spirits, other friends.

As you close the book and begin your own conversations, may I recall for your encouragement Paul's words to the Galatians, "You will harvest what you plant" (6:7). As you engage in conversations about simple living, you will be planting for a harvest that you may never experience—a world freed from its rush towards fearsome, nonsustainable selfishness. Because you have planted, though, a harvest *will* certainly occur. You have God's word on it.

God keep you joyful.

Resources

U se any of these resources to explore the subject of simplicity further. From among the scores of worthy candidates, I have recommended a handful of books, organizations, and Web sites that I think might be compelling or rewarding for you. The best list of resources, of course, is the one you assemble.

Books

Basye, Anne. *Sustaining Simplicity: A Journal.* Chicago, IL: Evangelical Lutheran Church in America, 2007.

Poet and author Anne Basye unlocks the cover of her personal journal about living simply. The entries reveal the inner struggles of a simplicity adherent, as well as the tenacious joy that enables the author's generosity, hospitality, and love for the people around her. *Sustaining Simplicity* provides an engaging look into the deeper meanings of simple living, which makes it a good catalyst for sharing in small groups.

⤜⤛

Collect and assess the messages in your junk mail for one week.
What about them is truly junk? What presumptions about you
(on the part of the mass mailer) caused this mail to reach your
eyes? How do you react to it, really?

⤜⤛

DeGrote-Sorensen, Barbara, and David Allen Sorensen. *'Tis a Gift to Be Simple: Embracing the Freedom of Living with Less.* Minneapolis: Augsburg Fortress, 1992.

This engaging book opens for appreciative scrutiny the life of a family trying to live simply inside of the difficult context of contemporary Western culture. The authors—one a teacher and freelance writer and the other a pastor—attracted strong attention in congregations with this book, their first attempt to take simplicity from a good idea to continuing habits of living. Practical at its heart, the book also inspires readers to try to find the gift of simple living in their own hearts.

Dungan, Nathan. *Prodigal Sons and Materials Girls: How Not to Be Your Child's ATM.* New York: John Wiley, 2003.

Dungan uses whimsy and straight talk to help parents gain skill in dealing with their children's developing sense of personal economics. The founder and president of Share+Save+Spend™, Dungan shares practical wisdom about successful parenting of teenagers who sorely need the skills and courage to use money wisely.

❦

Nothing is enough for the person for whom enough is too little.
—Epicurus

❦

Elgin, Duane. *Voluntary Simplicity: Toward a Way of Life That Is Outwardly Simple, Inwardly Rich.* New York: William and Morrow Company, 1993.

Probably among the handful of true classics in this field of knowledge, Duane Elgin's sourcebook (now in a revised edition) presents in powerful and elegant language the basic arguments for simplicity. Elgin's persuasive thoughts span the universe of simplicity philosophy, encompassing philosophy, economics, environmental concerns, sociology, and spirituality.

Lappé, Frances Moore, and Anna Lappé. *Hope's Edge: The Next Diet for a Small Planet.* New York: Jeremy P. Tarcher-Putnam, 2003.

One of the first activists to research and describe the dynamics of worldwide food distribution, author Frances Moore Lappé in this book documents her travels—with her daughter and coauthor Anna—to places in the world where small-scale food producers have held fiercely to the practices of justice. At first glance, you might think this book is not about simple living; in fact, *Hope's Edge* provides a global perspective on the effects of lifestyle decisions on the world's population. Courage, integrity, and tenacious insistence on justice characterize all the case studies the authors profile.

❧

A while back I received a mail circular inviting me to a seminar that would help me to live "rich and rowdy" after I turn 50. I'm wondering if I should accept the invitation, seeing as how I already have plenty of everything that's necessary and haven't colored inside the lines for years. And when I grow past 70, is "free and frisky" next?

❧

Schut, Michael, ed., comp. *Simpler Living, Compassionate Life: A Christian Perspective.* Denver: Living the Good News, 1999.

Writer-editor Schut collects in one volume some of the best thinking about simplicity from among its best thinkers. This aggregation of thought-provoking essays is accompanied by a study guide for groups and individuals. A good one-stop source for a comprehensive look at the simplicity movement.

Schumacher, E. F. *Small Is Beautiful: A Study of Economics as if People Mattered.* New York: HarperPerennial, 1989, c1973.

One of the first—and perhaps most enduring—books outlining the case for simplicity in its broadest definition, this classic work set the simplicity movement on its course toward broader appeal and acceptance by the thinking public. Even after more than 30 years, Schumacher's analysis still holds value for Christians who see Christ as countercultural or whose critique of present-day economics requires validation. A must-read for anyone beginning the journey toward simplicity.

~≈~

Late in their lives my parents started to give away their belong-
ings to my brothers and me. Most of their possessions were tattered
memorabilia, so their gifts became the inspiration for telling
family stories. Our memories will never be tattered.

~≈~

Simon, Arthur. *How Much Is Enough? Hungering for God in an*
Affluent Culture. Grand Rapids, MI: Baker Books, 2003.

In this his third book, Art Simon, founder and president
emeritus of Bread for the World scans the subject of simplicity
using a wide-angle lens. Developing the big picture of simplicity, Simon connects ideals and ideas in earnest, readable
language. Especially helpful are his poignant anecdotes and
his continuing references to the scriptural and doctrinal de-
terminants of simplicity. His writing mirrors his spirit: direct,
thoughtful, and humble.

Wheatley, Margaret J. *Turning to One Another: Simple Conversa-*
tions to Restore Hope to the Future. San Francisco: Berrett-Koehler
Publishers, Inc., 2002.

Since I first read them in 2002, Wheatley's insights have instructed me in conversation as method for social change, an
area of thought that has undergirded much of my thinking
and writing. Her practical view of conversation's value fills her
quiet book, as much a plea for what is truly important in life
as it is a treatise about social change.

Web Sites

Connect to any of these links to find organizations or enterprises already fully engaged in matters of simplicity. Some offer resources, others connectivity to people like you. (Hint: See the blogs at each site.) Remember that you are part of a growing cloud of witnesses that understands God's economy, God's will, God's love. When it comes to simplicity, you are never alone. Try these links to see how that works.

Alternatives for Simple Living: www.SimpleLiving.org. Alternatives@SimpleLiving.org (e-mail address); Alternatives for Simple Living, 109 Gaul Dr., PO Box 340, Sergeant Bluff, IA 51054; 800-821-6153 or 712-943-6153, Fax: 712-943-1402.

> This enterprise was begun more than 30 years ago by a co-alition of Christian denominations as a way to disseminate information and expertise about the simple-living movement. Since that beginning, Alternatives has continued to print its signature piece, *Whose Birthday Is It, Anyway?* in time for Advent each year. Its services continue to expand, as does its outreach to all people of faith, particularly young adults.

Holden Village: www.holdenvillage.org. Holden Village, HC0 Box 2, Chelan, WA 98816-9769; (The village has no on-site phone number).

> The programs and people of this year-round retreat center, located deep in the Cascades of Washington State, are con-sistently named as a regenerating experience for participants across the country. The long-standing commitment of Holden Village to principles of simplicity has made the center a favored locus for the personal transformation for many leaders, lay and clergy, and their families.

When my father died, I took care of the flowers question simply enough. In his death notice I characterized my father as a generous and loving man and directed possible flower donors to think of someone, still alive, who was also generous and loving, and to send them the flowers as a living memorial. My father would have liked the idea.

Simple Living America: www.simplelivingamerica.org. Simple Living America, P.O. Box 9955, Glendale, CA 91226; toll-free phone number: 1-877-UNSTUFF.

A project of the CRESP Center for Transformative Action at Cornell University, this Web site—and its associated services—is one of the cornerstone addresses for connectivity to the world of simplicity. A noteworthy feature: an online simple-living survey that is gradually turning into a reliable measure of simplicity. The site is also a primary connection to *Simple Living with Wanda Urbanska,* whose public television series has continued to grow in importance as a medium of instruction and encouragement in simplicity.

Take Back Your Time Day: www.timeday.org.

A major U.S.-Canada initiative that challenges the stubborn epidemic of overwork, overscheduling, and time famine that continues to threaten our brains and bodies, our families and relationships, our communities and environment. (So you know: October 24 is Take Back Your Time Day.)

The Simple Living Network: www.simpleliving.net; 800-318-5725.

One of the first and most highly respected organizations in the simplicity movement, The Simple Living Network draws together almost all of the major partners in the growing family of simplicity enterprises. The network's URL is one of the portals to the classic simplicity resource, *Your Money or Your Life*, and its associated benefits. Of special interest: the number of local simplicity circles operating around the country, with this organization as their hub. The bookstore offers a wide array of study and reading materials for use in groups and for individual reflection.

The Simplicity Forum: www.simplicityforum.org. The Simplicity Forum, PO Box 1812, Lyons, CO 80540; 303-747-6325.

A fascinating think tank of simplicity thinkers, including academics, artists, entrepreneurs, educators, activists, and authors. A good place to enter the world of simplicity that prospers outside of the church, the Simplicity Forum features a growing collection of research papers, unique Web addresses, and partnerships. The Simplicity Forum also sponsors periodic conferences that gather leaders in the national and international simplicity movement.